AF553735

FUNCTIONING OF AUTONOMOUS COLLEGES

FUNCTIONING OF AUTONOMOUS COLLEGES

By

VUPPUTURI PALA PRASADA RAO

M.A., M.Phil., M.Ed.

P.G.C.T.E.(CIEFL), (Ph.D.)

Lecturer in English

J.K.C. College

Guntur–522006

Andhra Pradesh

Editor

Dr. DIGUMARTI BHASKARA RAO

M.Sc., M.A., M.A., M.Ed., Ph.D.

Reader & Research Director

R.V.R. College of Education

Guntur–522006, India

digumartibhaskararao@rediffmail.com

DISCOVERY PUBLISHING HOUSE PVT. LTD.

NEW DELHI-110 002

First Published-2008

ISBN 978-81-8356-258-4

Published by:

DISCOVERY PUBLISHING HOUSE PVT. LTD.

4831/24, Ansari Road, Prahlad Street,
Darya Ganj, New Delhi-110002 (India)
Phone: 23279245 • Fax: 91-11-23253475
E-mail: dphbooks@rediffmail.com
dphtemp@indiatimes.com

Printed at.
Arora Offset Press
Laxmi Nagar, Delhi–92

Dedicated to Beloved

Dr. KONDABOLU BASAVAPUNNAIAH

An embodiment of discipline of order highest,
A Karmayogi who strives on and on hardest,
And still hardest to scale pinnacles of glory in all domains,
That one dreams of and nothing he remains
Unfulfilled, a practical idealist to the core,
And the posterity could hardly find such a one of yore.

PREFACE

Tertiary education, which follows twelve years of primary and secondary education, is popularly referred to as higher education. A nation's intellectual dynamism, resourcefulness and economic prosperity rely upon the quality of higher education. In the context of globalization, it is in the full glare of the media and the public. Almost every week, one comes across articles on it, most of which are highly critical. One of the constant refrains of the articles is how the systemic weaknesses debilitate higher education.

In fact, the present higher education system in India is conceptually a product of the colonial rule. It is clear that the British managed to subvert the system to run an exploitative empire. Naturally, the system is in no way pro-people in the parlance of modern democracy. It is neither generative of employment and empowerment nor conducive to entrepreneurship for business or industry. The crisis in higher education is not, in fact, a constraint of paucity of funds but of anachronistic academic practices. As a system advances, it has to shed its rigidity, increase its adaptability and respond to the emerging trends. Over the years Indian higher education behaves like a ponderous elephant, which cannot easily change its pace or direction. It defies any change. The affiliating universities, for instance, fail to live up to the expectations of a developing nation in no small measure. Right from the Higher Education Commission (1948-49), all the important commissions like the Education (Kothari) Commission (1964-66), the National Policy on Education (1986) Ramamurthy Committee Report (1990) and the Revised Programme of Action (1992) to list a few but critical ones, were unequivocal to decry affiliating system and suggested that college autonomy is one of the remedies to the evils pestering higher education.

When it comes to an affiliated college, curriculum design, teaching, learning and evaluation are common and are decided by the university. The college has a restricted option of choosing the courses. The affiliated system has been criticized on many counts. To list out a few, it is a legacy of the past, engineered by colonial masters to suit their interests. Barring the three nations in the sub-continent, India, Pakistan and Bangladesh, it is not in practice anywhere. However, when a college is granted autonomy it will decide what to and how to teach and evaluate. The college gets separated from the university, though not completely. Academic package will become flexible and the decision-making is internalized, changes and updating could be easily carried out, depending on the need as reflected from the feedback taken from alumni, user sectors, among others. Autonomy promotes academic culture unfettered from the shackles of affiliated system.

It is, however, baffling to understand the reasons for the aversion for autonomous system as evinced from some quarters of academic circles. Even though many universities directed colleges to go for autonomous system, most of the affiliated colleges have not ventured to embrace autonomy perhaps fearing that it would pose problems of governance. However, NACC has injected a new flow of ideas and enthusiasm into academic fraternity. In a way, it has empowered an accredited college to march ahead and pursue its mission with unflagging zeal. As a result, many colleges have shed their inveterate fear and are willing to opt for autonomy.

When it comes to the jurisdiction of Acharya Nagarjuna University, only two colleges, P.B. Siddhartha College, Vijayawada, and Andhra Loyola College, Vijayawada came forward to go for autonomy when the university proposed a scheme to this effect in the late 80s. These colleges had been performing well under affiliating system. For these colleges, however, autonomy seems to hold out a promise of excellence. It is remarkable that these colleges were wedded to autonomy when some other colleges of equally good repute were complacent in the cocoon of affiliated system. Now the question is how far they are able to translate the ideals of college autonomy as enshrined in the UGC guidelines. About two decades went by but most of the affiliated colleges are still in the rut of affiliating system and are not euphoric over college autonomy. Of late, a few more colleges such as Sri Durga Malleswara Siddhartha Mahila College, Vijayawada; Maris Stella College, Vijayawada; V.S.R & N.V.R. College, Tenali; Montessori Mahila College, Vijayawada; J.M.J. College of Women, Tenali; Noble College, Machilipatnam and St. Joseph's College of Education for Women, Guntur have switched over to college autonomy after accreditation by NACC. It is remarkable to note that there are quite a good number of other colleges which have shed fear and are ready to embrace the new system. But the colleges mentioned were not included in the sample since they are in the initial phases with the usual teething troubles.

It is incumbent on my part to elucidate the reasons for taking up this project. Many colleges are going to switch over to autonomous system and some have many nagging doubts about it. They have misgivings that the UGC scheme of college autonomy is aimed at commercializing higher education, reducing government funding and encouraging only marketable education at the expense of liberal arts and basic sciences. The informed view is that if the government is going to waive aid to autonomous institutions, the possibility of stopping the aid will also hang over the affiliated colleges like a sword of Damocles. In this context, it may be borne in mind the Human Resource Minister, Arjun Singh's statement in Lok Sabha who, while dispelling suspicions, clarified that autonomy would enable a college to obtain increased allocation of funds from the UGC for its faculty improvement, functional orientation and overall development. The academicians continue to be sceptical about such a lasting benevolent stand towards funding higher educational institutions. In fact, this is one of the reasons for looking at the college autonomy with an air of suspicion.

Teacher unions are staunch opponents of the scheme. I attended a seminar on college autonomy at a college in Guntur, at the end of which all the lecturers with one accord vehemently opposed college autonomy when a proposal was mooted seeking their views. My experience was no different in another college where the discussion on college autonomy met with a similar fate.

All this lends credence that though College Autonomy has many feathers in its cap in principle, it suffers from some shortcomings in practice. Furthermore, it can be seen that there is a glaring gap in academic research in the area of functioning of autonomous system. It is in these contexts that I have embarked upon this project to study and unravel various problems and propose some suggestions for the successful functioning of college autonomy.

It goes without saying that college autonomy, as a corrective to the affiliating system, should not degenerate into old wine in an old bottle with a new label. Autonomy for a college implies that the college and its teachers assume responsibility for the academic programmes they provide, for the content and quality of their teaching and for admission and assessment of their students. In order to generate enthusiasm and enlightened awareness and set the scene for college autonomy, workshops and seminars have to be organized to prevail upon the staff and students whose whole-hearted participation is a must for the success of college autonomy. In the same breath, workshops and training programmes need to be organized for the non-teaching staff. Such multi-pronged preparation is indispensable because the institution has to gear up its machinery to perform many of the functions, which the university has hitherto performed.

When autonomy is granted, the stakeholders cannot afford to be self-complacent. In order to make it a resounding success, the teaching staff in the main should be keen on updating their pedagogic skills and be collaborative in their academic endeavours. Furthermore, academic audit, constant orientation and periodic overhaul of the system will ensure the successful functioning of college autonomy. When there are glaring loopholes in an affiliating university in terms of syllabi design, conducting examinations and valuation, the public and media are quick to find fault with the system. In a way, they are helpful in either correcting the erring individuals or suggesting ways to ameliorate the system. However, such news about an autonomous institution may escape the public or media's attention because it is relatively small. It may peter out without being noticed!

Of the many determinants which pave way for success of autonomous system, collaboratively-structured efforts are of prime importance. The obvious fact is that the inter-personal relationships of the individuals working in an autonomous college are crucial. It is clear that an autonomous system entails collective endeavours, and hence, its success necessitates harmonious inter-personal relationships. Lone individual brilliance, isolated efforts and lack of rapport among the individuals and unhealthy professional rivalry prove to be detrimental and they are bound to tell upon the tenor of the autonomous institution. Herein lays the importance of the principal whose breadth of vision, infallible judgment, unprejudiced assessment of individuals and above all, his qualities of head and heart go a long way in making autonomy a resounding success. It can be rounded off with a touch of certainty that united the system stands, divided it falls.

To conclude, college autonomy as a system is viable and has many advantages. Nevertheless, individuals are an inseparable part of it and therefore, are the heart of a system. It is upon their shoulders that the success of the system rests. To put it squarely, individuals can either make or mar the system. Like many other good systems, College Autonomy will fail to realize the enshrined objectives if individuals go bankrupt of ideas and are lacking in sincerity of purpose, intellectual dynamism and above all, discipline. If the stakeholders go wrong, then it is not the failure of the system but the collective inadequacy of the individuals. A system prospers or becomes puerile because of the individuals who are the crux of it.

The onerous task of the project, spanned over a good number of years, has been undertaken to enable the teaching community in particular to have a fair knowledge of many benchmark practices enumerated in the study. It is earnestly hoped that this modest study will cater to the needs of those working in various capacities in autonomous and non-autonomous colleges.

Prasada Rao

Bhaskara Rao

Of the many determinants which [illegible] for success of autonomous system, collectively structured efforts are of prime importance. The driving force is that the [illegible] of deliberations, plans and actions [illegible]. In an autonomous college [illegible] system [illegible] enthusiastic [illegible] involved [illegible] among the individuals and [illegible] professionals [illegible] of the institution and they [illegible] upon the [illegible] autonomous institution [illegible] of a system [illegible] above [illegible] a long way in making autonomy a reality [illegible] with a [illegible] the system stands, divided it falls.

To conclude, college autonomy [illegible] many advantages. Nevertheless, individuals [illegible] and separately [illegible] and therefore, are the heart of a system. It is upon their shoulders that the success of the system rests. To such a state individuals [illegible] make or mar the system. [illegible] autonomous college, autonomy will fail to realise its cherished [illegible] if individuals [illegible] of [illegible] intellectual dynamism, [illegible] above all discipline [illegible] of the system, but the collective [illegible] the system prospers or becomes [illegible] because of the individuals who are [illegible].

The original idea of this project [illegible] of which has been [illegible] to enable [illegible] practices [illegible] in the study. It is [illegible] that this study will [illegible] both [illegible] autonomous and non-autonomous colleges.

CONTENTS

1

INTRODUCTION

There is a general consensus among the academics that the state of Indian higher education is far from satisfactory. The impression is that standards are on the decline and that the knowledge and skills being imparted by the institutions are to a great extent irrelevant to the needs of a vibrant society. The failure of the system to live up to expectations and aspirations of the nation has been attributed to a host of causes including its colonial roots, the failure to control unplanned expansion, perennial paucity of funds, inflexible academic structure with an antiquated system resisting all changes, politicized and bureaucratized systems of governance, the distancing of the universities and a general lack of concern. In his article on *The Crisis in Higher Education* brought out in The Hindu, R. Ramachandra Rao (2007) spoke in the same vein, saying that there is "quiet crisis" in higher education. The centres of undoubted quality, like Indian Institutes of Technology, Indian Institutes of Management and some universities and colleges, co-exist with colleges that are in a stagnated state. A bird's eye-view of the overall situation has been described as "the existence of islands of excellence in a sea of mediocrity".

It was Charles Wood's Dispatch in 1854 which gave the idea of establishing universities in India on the model of the London University. The Dispatch described the aim of Indian education as the diffusion of arts, science, philosophy, literature of Europe and the study of Indian languages. The three Presidency universities founded in 1857 at three port towns—Calcutta,

Bombay and Madras—were the first set of centres of higher learning in the sub-continent. For decades the colleges which remained affiliated to the universities were allowed to perform the soulless task of "covering the course", prescribed by some external agency i.e., a university. With its legendary English flavour, the university affiliating system was accompanied by a multiplicity of bodies steeped in a colonial mindset and steadily bureaucratized over the years. Independent India thus inherited a system of higher education which was "impregnated with colonial seeds and wedded to the achievement of colonial objectives".

The Limitations of Affiliated Colleges

It is interesting to note that other than India, Pakistan and Bangladesh no other country has the affiliating mode in higher education. The University of London was adopted as the model in 1854. It was then a university of the affiliating type and was good as an examining body but it could not safeguard standards of achievement. The British government was eager to oversee complete sway over education and therefore imposed upon India uniformity in the sphere of higher education. All Indians were in favour of the uniformity because it held out the promise of financial supporting in the form of grant-in-aid. Quite naturally native opinion only dealt upon the benefits of the system. Even after the attainment of independence, the confidence in the potency of English education is still largely unshaken. In the same pattern affiliated system prospers, growing by leaps and bounds causing concern among academic circles. What the Viceroy, Lord Curzon in 1901 while addressing the educational Conference at Simla, is relevant today: "We started by a too slavish imitation of English models, and to this day we have never purged ourselves of the taint." Thus the cramping system had taken deep roots among the people of India, shaping their minds and thoughts to an extent greater than what Macaulay anticipated the Employment Exchanges in the country are indicative.

During the first years of its independence, the country witnessed an unprecedented expansion of the higher education. It began with 20 universities in 1947. The figure rose to about 300.

Similarly the number of the colleges rose from 700 to 16,000. The undergraduate system constitutes 80 per cent of the higher education system in India. Most of these undergraduate colleges are of the nature of affiliated colleges. The problems confronted by affiliated colleges are many and varied. Higher education is basically a pursuit of excellence. A few colleges, which have gained laurels, were treated alike with the rest of the other substandard colleges by the parent university. The same treatment meted out to all the colleges is unjust because they are not uniform in size of staff, students, the mission of management and academic performance and infrastructure. The cramping system of the university does not recognize the unique character of the institutions performing at various levels under its jurisdiction. As a result, they have been bulldozed into a state of uniform mediocrity. This has made the academic mindset lapse into a state of inertia with no initiative being taken to introduce new disciplines or abandon the courses that have become outdated and irrelevant.

M. Aruchami's observation on the affiliating system is noteworthy. It has "changed the university into an examination conducting body, converted the colleges into tutorial institutions and the teachers into tutors." It has eliminated initiative, leadership and involvement from the academic community rendering the academic atmosphere both rigid and archaic. In consequence, teaching-learning which is the essence of transmission of wisdom and skill has become a symbolic examination qualifying process. Further, the university by virtue of its insularity and legislative autonomy places itself outside the scope of public accountability and its teaching staff has a limited stake in the quality or progress of the system.

Moreover, the bulging registers of huge workforce of unemployable degree holders. Their ranks swell year after year as the colleges that produce them go on turning out their half-baked products. Their degree does not conform to the elementary rules of the market forces that operate ruthlessly outside the precincts of the colleges. Thus the affiliating system with its limitations and inadequacies fail to generate batches of young women and men capable of meeting with the new demands in the ever expanding branches of learning.

Some Exceptions

As a centralized system, affiliated system has some advantages. For instance, there is a certain degree of standardization in the courses of study and uniformity in assessment. These features will be helpful to the prospective employees. Moreover, the representatives of the colleges in Academic Councils can effect changes in the syllabi, examination pattern and evaluation. It can be seen that on one side there are many institutions that find fault with the universities and remain stagnant. While on the other, there are "a few self-motivated institutions" that initiate programmes on their own. For instance, St.Xavier's College of Mumbai, an affiliate of Mumbai University, offers various courses in the afternoon. On fulfilling the requirements of the course, the students obtain a certificate from the college which is valued high in the job market. It is able to utilize its infrastructure to the maximum extent.

Barring isolated examples, however, there is no congenial academic atmosphere for the development of the colleges wedded to affiliated system. It was not without reason that Lord Curzon disparaged the affiliating system saying that it "did more harm than good." It is only wishful thinking that an affiliated college can be as successful as an autonomous one given the inherent limitations of an affiliate. Hence, the Radhakrishnan Commission wanted the affiliating system "to disappear from the Indian landscape at the earliest possible moment."

The Kothari Commission, nevertheless, recognized that affiliating universities were indestructible and suggested a compromise. More than 30 colleges in close proximity should be affiliated to a university with a strong core of teaching departments. It also recommended college autonomy should be given impetus to the institutions far flung. But 40 years later, affiliated colleges and universities continue to multiply. The entire system became a huge machine for manufacturing degree holders and clerks and in which little attention was paid to moral training, creativity, and other finer aspects of culture. There is a consensus among the academicians of various committees viewed that affiliated system has many failings. They feel that college autonomy would address the problems galore. True, the affiliating system was devised to regulate and standardize the quality of education. But with the tremendous increase in the number of institutions and in the context of globalization, the system has become counter productive. Further, some substandard colleges serenely ride piggyback on the reputation of the parent university. It is a drag on the better institutions that would otherwise regularly revise and update their curricula and introduce innovative programmes. In order to allow growth and development, the autonomous college scheme was devised.

College Autonomy

If one looks it up in the Advanced Learner's Dictionary, the word, autonomy has two meanings: 1) (of an organization) "able to govern itself or control its own affairs" and 2) "able to make decisions without help from anyone else." To put it squarely, "freedom and self-rule" are the crux of autonomy. The concept of autonomy stands for freedom as this underpins scores of practices and ideals in a democratic society. It arises from the conviction that educational institutions conferred upon autonomy will achieve their aims and objectives better. The word has many connotations. In Sweezy vs. New Hampshire case, the U.S. Supreme Court defined four constituents of essential freedom bestowed upon a college: to determine who may teach, what may be taught and how and who may be admitted to study. Nevertheless, the acquired freedom should be nurtured in all earnestness so as to achieve social relevance and academic excellence.

It is interesting to note that autonomous system was rooted in ancient India. Ancient higher education institutions, Nalanda, Vikramshila, Vallabhi and Takshashila were essentially autonomous in character. They worked out their programmes without external control. The same trend of autonomous character of institutions continued during the medieval times. There was no slavish dependence. However, with the advent of the British, such practices gave place to affiliating mode authored by the colonial masters. The mode safeguarded their interests and it was easier to govern the institutions from a centre.

The idea of autonomous colleges, however, was mooted by R.K.Singh, Principal of Balwant Rajput College, Agra in 1953. Following his recommendations, an amendment was passed by the senate of the Agra University in 1954 but no college in the university applied for the autonomous status. In 1965, Prof S.K. Sidhanta Committee proposed the autonomous scheme as an alternative and as a corrective to the affiliating system. However, the first formal and specific recommendation for college autonomy appeared in the Kothari Commission report, 1964-66.

"Where there is an outstanding college (or a small cluster of very good colleges) within a large university, which has shown the capacity to improve itself markedly, consideration should be given to granting it an autonomous status. This would involve the power to frame its own rules of admission, to prescribe its courses of study, to conduct examinations and so on."

It has been, therefore, advocated that at least 10 per cent of the total colleges should be conferred autonomous status so that colleges can embark upon educational innovation. Had the Kothari Commission's norm of granting autonomy to at least ten per cent of the 11,000 colleges in the country been carried out in letter and spirit, there would have been nearly 1,100 autonomous colleges in the country today. However, there are only around 248 autonomous colleges by 2006 representing a major failure in the implementation of the policy. Even the National Policy on Education (NPE 1986) noted that the autonomous colleges will be helped to develop in large number until the affiliating system is replaced by autonomous colleges in a free and creative association with universities.

In 1973, the University Grants Commission sent a circular to all the universities recommending that they should pursue policies for converting affiliated colleges into autonomous ones. In 1974, the All India Association for Christian Higher Education organized a seminar at Delhi where various aspects of autonomy was examined exhaustively and considered in detail all problems and opportunities that autonomy might produce.

It was in those times that a renowned academician, Malcom Adiseshaiah took the reins of the University of Madras. He urged several colleges to prepare and submit proposal for autonomy by 1975. By the end of 1978 twelve colleges in the University of Madras and four in Madurai Kamaraj University started functioning. At the end of the first five-year term, all autonomous colleges in Tamil Nadu had been a success.

However, popularization of college autonomy got a major boost in the National Policy on Education (NPE) in 1986. The policy talked of replacing the system of affiliating by the system of autonomous colleges. It also makes provision "to enable autonomous colleges to award their own degrees" and for this purpose, if necessary to confer deemed university status on them. It has proposed to make 500 autonomous colleges by the end of Seventh Plan. In 1973, 1987, 1993, 1995 and 1998 the UGC issued guidelines on the scheme of autonomous colleges wherein it talked at length on the various aspects of college autonomy. Its document on the Tenth Plan clearly states that colleges with academic and operative freedom are doing better and have more credibility. Encouraged by the assistance given by the UGC and the euphoria generated in the post-accreditation phase in particular and enamoured of the benefits accrued, some colleges switched over to the system. They made significant strides in the realm of higher education.

Autonomous Colleges and Their Achievements

It is important to recognize that the case for autonomy of institutions rests on the fundamental consideration that higher education becomes meaningful when institutions both universities and colleges effectively discharge their principal functions of teaching, research and service to the community. Only an autonomous institution, free from regimentation of ideas can pursue the objectives undauntedly and build up a spirit of enquiry in its teachers and students. Habits of independent thinking and a spirit of enquiry unfettered by the limitations and prejudices are essential for the harmonious development of an institution at tertiary level. Where independent thinking dies out, there the weeds of authoritarianism stunts the growth of healthy academic life.

There is no gainsaying the fact that autonomous system has many merits. Autonomous scheme can weed out weak colleges, ensure enhancement of quality and put an end to the affiliating system since the institutions, London, Oxford and Cambridge universities which authored this novice, have themselves shed the concept after converting each college into an independent and self-contained unit. The various dilemmas confronting Indian society require vibrant and dynamic institutions of higher education, which can address social needs by creatively generating intellectual resources, using the freedom allowed to autonomous colleges. There is ample evidence after assessment of the performance of autonomous colleges that all the apprehensions against autonomy are speculative and without supporting evidence. The merits of autonomy detailed below far outweigh some shortcomings in the operational management of the system. It has been held that the autonomous colleges have been rated high in all the seven criteria posited by the NAAC, is itself a testimony of their inherent strength. It is worthwhile to see that the precursors of college autonomy in Acharya Nagarjuna University area, Andhra Loyola College secured the coveted "College with Potential for Excellence" status and the huge funds it accompanied in 2006; P.B. Siddhartha College is on its way to obtain the CPE status. There are some other autonomous institutions which have made great strides. Of these, colleges like Loyola College, Chennai deserve a note of appreciation. *India Today* magazine in 2006 magazine rated it as one of the top ten colleges in India. In Science, the college secured first rank, third in Arts, and third in Commerce. The Peer Team of NAAC re-accredited the College at A+ level in October, 2006 and the Quality Profile is 91. It is worthwhile to note here that it changed over to autonomy in 1978.

In consonance with the Guidelines brought out by the UGC, most of the autonomous colleges have been successful in introducing innovations in their academic programmes and educational technology thereby making students' academic endeavours more meaningful and purposive. Secondly, unlike in most of the affiliating universities, review and redesigning of programmes is systematically done through the Boards of Studies and Academic Council in autonomous colleges for proper management of academic affairs. The members of these bodies, apart from the faculty of the college, belong to all walks of life—experts from the industry, representatives of the university and the government.

Over the last few decades, there have been remarkable changes in the educational system in India and many of these changes have taken place in the sphere of curriculum. Of these, the credit based system merits attention. It has been in vogue in the USA for the last four decades and it has been adopted by many a prestigious institution like the IITs, IIMs, NITs and some Central Universities. In this system, the learner-oriented approach to learning is stressed. They are given free hand to pursue an integrated programme at their own pace in keeping with their ability and aptitude. This system provides broad-based education with greater flexibility in the choice of courses. Further, it enables highly motivated and talented students to gain extra credits as it gives scope to students to get along at their own pace. Affiliated colleges cannot embrace this new pattern as they have to follow scrupulously the curriculum structure conceived by the university. On the other hand, many autonomous colleges have successfully designed the cafeteria model of choice-based credit system, which allows every student to construct his or her own curriculum structure in accordance with his/her aptitude, interest and career plans. In fact, the success of this concept has encouraged other colleges to opt for autonomy along with the credit system.

In consonance with their objectives, autonomous colleges have been able to introduce compulsory course on value education thereby moulding students' personality. The affiliating system, on the other hand, has failed to cater to the fundamental need to impart value education to their students. Autonomous colleges will turn into competing class of institutions and so students have choice to pursue their goals with vision and vigour in the congenial atmosphere. Autonomous colleges have an impressive record of enriching the syllabi and preparing the students for various competitive exams. They have enhanced placement and self-employment opportunities, meaningful interaction between institution and industry thereby enabling the students to go for employment avenues. Furthermore, autonomous colleges have successfully implemented various evaluation techniques in the examination system. The continuous assessment, which forms an integral part of the colleges, propels students to work hard consistently. Moreover, the colleges have proved that there is no limit to the creativity of pedagogical techniques and the teaching learning process substantially enriched by creating a challenging, participative, and highly interactive learning environment. Moreover, opportunities, which enhance employability like job experience, project work, have helped the student assimilate skills along with his/her degree thereby making the process of learning a very satisfying experience. It can be seen from the merits of autonomous colleges that apart from innovation in teaching, learning and customization in course content, they are able to continuously change their approach and methods to cope with the contemporary global scenario.

Autonomous Colleges and Their Limitations

It is far from truth, however, to say that autonomous colleges do not have any inadequacies and systemic weaknesses. It is a fact that in the practice of authority, power and influence has its own role to play in the institutions of higher education. Sometimes college autonomy is a smokescreen for the authorities concerned to exercise power over others to promote vested interests. While some relish freedom, many do not know what autonomy has brought forth. Little do they know the very concept and hence cannot take part in the transactions meaningfully. In other words, there exist differences between "autonomy in principle and in practice; intended autonomy and implemented autonomy; expected autonomy and exercised autonomy and experienced autonomy." The autonomous institutions have to function with the social and political orders. For example, in India universities enjoy advantages of academic freedom in principle. In practice, their autonomy is sharply qualified by the exigencies of administrative, governmental and financial external controls and internal university administration. Though the universities are free to devise courses of their choice, their ability to implement the courses depend on the external controls, for example, faculty appointments, teacher training, building grants and developmental grants. In order to secure them, the colleges have to meet government and regulatory bodies endorsed criteria.

Perhaps, the problems of the autonomous colleges outnumber those of the universities. Autonomous colleges have to abide by the norms of (i) the Universities as they give the degrees and approvals for courses (ii) the State governments as they finance the salary of the staff and (iii) the UGC and Ministry of Human Resource Development as they give developmental grants, intake, etc., All these constitute layers of administrative controls, which at times interfere with the autonomy of a college.

Further, autonomy is not something that gets implemented in the institutions by making provisions in the acts and statutes or for that matter, by mere granting freedom by the regulatory bodies or central and state governments. Rather, it is the individuals as heads within the institutions, who matter more in the actual exercise of autonomy. The success indicators of autonomy are that (a) the decisions of the institution are taken with the participation of the employees of the institution; for the benefit of the stakeholders, the programmes are implemented by the institution and these are supported by the State, Centre and other regulatory bodies based on (b) the outcome of the above, further decisions are to be taken and implemented by the institutions to ensure quality. (c) Another indicator is that clarity with regard to the working partnership of different agencies controlling and contributing directly or indirectly to the institutions, viz. central and state governments, regulatory bodies and funding agencies and d) quality assurance of its programmes and accountability of its academic, non-academic staff and its management towards tax payers and stakeholders.

There is another danger inherent in the concept of autonomy. With each autonomous college having its own syllabi, there will be multitude of standards each non-comparable with others. As a result, many universities would not like to consider the inclusion of the students of autonomous colleges in the list of university ranks. The issue kicked up a row at the Academic Council Meeting at Madurai Kamaraj University brought out in The Hindu on the

20th June, 2005. Moreover, there is danger of divisive tendencies making inroads into syllabi. Autonomous colleges would find themselves small in terms of academic resource personnel to undertake the task and the target laid down. Further, the system may lead to competitive jacking up of examination scores in order to spruce up the image of an institution. It has been observed that in some colleges, the teaching community is so complacent that it keeps syllabi largely unmodified. It is pertinent to observe that an institution does need congenial atmosphere and its teachers should be endowed with qualities like commitment and integrity. Mere autonomous status would not enable a college to be good at everything without consistent creative and committed efforts. It can be noted that many universities are not good though they are autonomous.

STATEMENT OF THE PROBLEM

An Analytical Study of the Functioning of Autonomous Colleges.

OBJECTIVES OF THE STUDY

The objectives of the present study are set forth below:

1. To find out and analyze the whole range of problems being confronted in autonomous colleges in Vijayawada;
2. To identify the strengths of autonomous colleges;
3. To make the students specify the problems in the functioning of autonomous colleges;
4. To unravel principals' and lecturers' stance towards the focal problems and functioning of autonomous colleges;
5. To draw the suggestions from principals, lecturers and students and to know different problems of college autonomy and to suggest measures to resolve the problems.

RESEARCH QUESTIONS

The researcher has formulated the following research questions to test their validity in the light of the data collected:

1. Do the principals belonging to a minority autonomous college and an open–category autonomous college differ on various issues regarding autonomous system?
2. Do the lecturers belonging to various faculties differ on various issues regarding autonomous system?
3. Do the students belonging to various disciplines differ on various issues regarding autonomous system?

SCOPE OF THE STUDY

The study is aimed to investigate only the functioning of the two autonomous colleges and hence it is highly confined. The present study is designed to study the problems of different persons involved in the system of college autonomy—principals, lecturers, and students—in either implementing autonomous system or watching the problems at the receiving end. This study is limited to the autonomous colleges in Acharya Nagarjuna University (ANU) though the suggestions inferred from the data can be applied to the other institutions of similar nature.

NEED OF THE STUDY

Autonomous colleges have come to stay in the realm of higher education. They represent a very radical departure from the existing structure of the university system—a system, which is a product of distortions and consequences of an outmoded affiliating system. Autonomy, in principle, enables a college to develop and propose programmes that are considered relevant to its immediate environment as well as to the country as a whole. In other words, an autonomous college should be able to identify the aspirations of the community around it and also the demands of job-market and effectively translate those aspirations.

However, it has been felt that the autonomous colleges at least to some extent fail to realize the ideal for which they have come into existence. There seems to be lack of rapport between the university and the colleges. Though the problems posed by the A.P. State Council of Higher Education and the U.G.C. are not many they are very significant. Many an academician feels that unless the problems are resolved to make the system function smoothly, the system might not deliver goods. It is for these reasons that the researcher took up the area of the autonomous colleges in Vijayawada, which are under the jurisdiction of Acharya Nagarjuna University.

2

REVIEW OF RELATED LITERATURE

Review of related literature is crucial because the researcher is supposed to be familiar with the studies that have gone before in the area. A survey of related studies implies locating, studying and evaluating reports of relevant researches, study of published articles, going through related portions of encyclopaedias and research abstracts, study of pertinent pages out of comprehensive books on the subject and going through related manuscripts if any. For any worthwhile study in any field of knowledge the researcher needs an adequate familiarity with the work, which has already been done in the area of his choice. He needs to acquire up-to-date information about what has been thought and done in that particular area.

Research takes the advantage of the knowledge, which has accumulated in the past as a result of constant human endeavour. It can never be undertaken in isolation of the work that has already been done on the problems of which are directly related to study proposed by a researcher. A review of the related literature must precede well-planned research study.

The review of the literature is an important part of the scientific approach and is carried out in all areas of scientific research, whether in the physical, natural or social sciences. Such reviews also form the basis of most research in the humanities. The review of the literature in educational research provides with the means of getting to the frontier in a particular field of knowledge until the researcher has learned what others have done and what remains still to be done in his area. Thus, the literature in any field forms the foundation upon which all future works must be built. The researcher, however, should make every effort to complete a thorough review before starting his research because the insight and knowledge gained by the review almost inevitably lead to a better-designed project and greatly improve the chances of obtaining important and significant results. Often, the insights gained through the review will save the researcher time and money. Further, a summary of the writings of recognized authorities and of previous research provides evidence that the researcher is familiar with what is already known and what is still unknown and untested. Since effective research is based upon past knowledge, this step helps to eliminate the duplication of what has been done and provides useful hypotheses and helpful suggestions for significant investigation. Citing studies that show substantial agreement and those that seem to present conflicting conclusions, help to sharpen and define understanding of existing knowledge in the problem area, provide a background for the research project, and make the reader aware of the status of the issue.

Although the general purpose of review is to help the researcher develop thorough understanding and an insight into previous work and the trends that have emerged, the review can also help in reaching a number of important specific goals.

RESEARCH STUDIES

The following are the different areas on which research studies on the area in question had been carried out:

Machy, D.L. (1960) in an investigation on the relationship between diversity and freedom concluded that they are inter-related. Diversity, which results in excellence, is the key to freedom. Freedom involves choice. Choice presupposes diversity of things from which to choose. What most protects freedom of choice in America is the great diversity of its institutions, none of which have overriding power. The structure of American higher education exemplifies this. Its liberty is buttressed by the variety of its institutions. No arbitrary pattern, no central pattern, has ever been imposed. The diversity of the system offers the student a multitude of choices. The institutions of his choice may be operated under either public or private control; it may be affiliated to a church, or it may be non-sectarian. The student may choose an institution to fit his intellectual capacity as well as his interests.

In fact the diversified system of higher education is capable of producing not only what John Gardner, President of Carnegie Corporation, has referred to as the "brilliant men at the top, but also excellently trained second, third, forth and fifth level of workers."

Alvin C. Eurich (1963) studied educational experiments in American colleges and universities offering the matrix of historical perspectives. He says that American tradition of higher education is one of local autonomy, diversity, and innovation. Freedom to experiment has, of course, been the source of both strengths and weaknesses in American colleges and universities, but at its best it has encouraged genuine progress.

American colleges entered the 20th century riding the crest of a wave of curriculum innovation. The great experiment of 19th century the elective system allowing students to choose their own pattern of courses, had reached its peak. The elective system triumphed because the spectacular growth in scientific knowledge had undermined the tacit assumption of liberal classical arts education and that the student during his college career could cover the whole range of basic human knowledge. Finding these no longer possible, American colleges had swung to the other extreme of at least assuring that each student became a competent specialist. However, some felt that they failed to provide a firm grounding in common intellectual and spiritual heritage.

Owing to the autonomous nature of American colleges, a number of colleges intensively experimented on the curriculum design in the 20th century. In 1945, this movement has climaxed and codified in Harward University's famous report, "General Education in a Free Society" which established a pattern that has since become dominant on American campuses. Under the system, specialization is provided through many elective courses but every student is required to take a solid core of basic liberal studies. Some American colleges rejected the elective system as well as its predecessor, the rigid classical curriculum, because neither seemed to provide for the student's 'total development' as a human being. These progressive institutions sought to give each student a unified programme designed for his individual needs and capacities. Other American colleges inaugurated different types of programmes. Reed College tried to focus student's energies on academic matters by de-emphasizing the non-academic activities, which characterize most campuses. The University of Cincinnati and Borea College demonstrated the effectiveness of students after noting periods of academic study and practical experience. Stephens College built its curriculum around the actual problems that its women students were likely to meet in adult life. It is clear that experimentation has given American education vitality and diversity, which can only ensure in autonomous institutions through their unique way of fashioning curriculum. One factor had a decisive effect upon their character. All were under local control. Each had its own management. For over two centuries or more, there was not even any association to require or even influence them toward uniformity. This freedom of chalking out their own academic programme opens the way not only for striking advances, but also for abuse. The power to adapt to local circumstances sometimes went too far. There was a strong tendency for example, to scrap foreign language, Mathematics, the sciences and the rigorous academic disciplines generally. In their effort to be genuinely democratic and to provide academic training for nearly every vocation, many institutions diluted their scholastic standards.

In his study on American Education, Joseph F. Kauffman (1966) while writing at length on higher education says that there is no national system of higher education in the U.S.A. if by 'system' people means a uniform body of institution with a similar programmes, standard and financial support. Instead, there are over 2,100 separate institutions ranging from two-year 'junior' colleges (two years beyond the secondary level like in Andhra Pradesh) to complex universities, and from technical institutions to classical liberal arts colleges. The maze of institutions beyond the high school has been characterized by W.H. Cowley, an authority on the development of American education, as a sprawling, complex a diversified mingle-mangle. Church groups, ethnic groups, cities and states all established or influenced institutions of higher education. The diversity and cultured pluralism of American life are thus reflected in this variety of colleges and universities.

Sudha Rao, K. (1999) studied the problems related to autonomy, administration and quality. According to him, there is positive relationship between autonomy and quality. Invariably 'administration gains power over autonomy' through the process aspects of implementation of policies at all levels. As per the norms of autonomous institutions, faculty is supposed to enjoy rights and privileges of academic decision-making but in practice, either in the name of parity of autonomous and non-autonomous colleges under the same university or in the guise of administrative norms and conditions of administration, status quo continues. Academic faculty feels constrained within the rigid structures. He suggested that the roles of regulatory bodies that are directly controlling autonomous institutions should be defined so that conflicting interests could be avoided and complementariness could be promoted. He concluded that change for the better was the only saving grace as far as autonomous colleges were concerned. Initiative on the part of an autonomous college is very crucial to tide over many problems.

THEORETICAL PERSPECTIVES

The following studies and reports help one acquaint with various theoretical perspectives in the area.

At the Workshop held at Chennai (1995) the principals of autonomous colleges admitted that all the colleges face constraints in implementing the spirit of autonomy conferred upon them. 1. They confront with many problems because the restricting clauses in the use of allotted funds as well as the delay in the release of funds by the UGC. 2. The indirect constraint imposed by the state government through the delay in the appointment of adequate number of teaching or non-teaching staff. Lack of staff both teaching and non-teaching erodes the efficiency of the autonomous structure. 3. The autonomous colleges have to abide by the rules of the government in the retirement of teachers, thereby blocking the selection of a specialist giving him financial incentive to each new area of studies. 4. The colleges are unable to offer new courses and degrees without the concurrence of the parent university. Of late, some universities have began to levy huge endowment fees on the courses of study in all colleges indirectly trying to halt many well-established colleges from starting innovative programmes, as they cannot find the extra funds to pay such courses. 5. The university administration through its apex bodies such as Syndicate and the Senate is often not fully in tune with the spirit of the functioning of autonomous colleges. There is constant interference imposing uniformity and dictating patterns of conformity. 6. Some universities have sanctioned autonomy only to UG courses leaving PG and M.Phil courses. 7. Any casual observer will easily take note of the increase in paper-work involving maintenance of records with regard to continuous assessment, periodic evaluation, attendance, preparation of annual reports and other. Further the semester system with continuous assessment increases the workload of the staff. The additional quantum of work is to be noted by the State Government, while fixing workload pattern and autonomous college need separate norms of workload. 8. The meritorious students in these colleges are sore when their ranks are not considered for awards in the list of university ranks. 9. Credibility of the internal assessment is often questioned. 10. For the effective functioning of the autonomous system, many statutory and non-statutory committees have been provided by the UGC. Most of the representatives to these committees nominated by the UGC, State Government and University lack the knowledge of the working of the autonomous system. 11. Added to this is the tales of woe from Autonomous Government Colleges, where teachers are constantly are on transfer, thus affecting continuity. None doubt the merits of autonomous colleges. But a number of problems crop up in its implementation. Unless these problems are addressed and resolved, the whole system may tumble down.

The U.G.C. Document on Autonomous Colleges (1998) dealt with all the aspects of autonomous college in a comprehensive fashion. It stated that autonomy is conferred on a college to achieve certain objectives that would make its academic programmes more sensible and socially relevant. The following are the objectives as laid down by the U.G.C (1998). An autonomcus college will have freedom to determine its own courses of study and syllabi, to evolve methods of evaluation and to conduct its own examinations as a means to achieve higher standards and greater creativity. It has also freedom to make use of modern tools of educational technology to achieve higher standards. Further, it can prescribe rules for admission in consonance with reservation policy of the State Government.

(i) Relationship with the Parent University and the State Government

Beset with the problems like notification of results and other non-academic issues the university and the affiliated college cannot strike meaningful chord in their relationship. However, autonomous colleges are free to make use of the expertise of university departments and other institutions to chalk out their curricula, devise methods of teaching, examination and evaluation. It helps the college develop academic programmes, improve the faculty and provide necessary guidance by participating in the deliberations of the different bodies of the college. The Parent University will promote academic freedom in autonomous colleges:

(a) By extending the freedom to colleges to introduce innovative academic programmes;

(b) To facilitate offering of new courses of study subject to the required minimum number of hours of instruction, content and standards;

(c) Not charging heavy payments towards endowments for the introduction of new courses of study;

(d) Permitting them to issue their own Provisional, Migration and other certificates;

(e) By doing everything possible to foster the spirit of autonomy.

(ii) The state government will assist the autonomous colleges by:

(a) avoiding, as far as possible, transfers of teachers, especially in colleges where academic innovation and reforms are in process;

(b) considering adaptation of a differential work-load pattern in order to recognize and encourage additional work involved in the exercise of autonomy; and

(c) conveying its concurrence for the extension of autonomy of any college to the commission within the stipulated time, i.e. 90 days after the receipt of the report of the review committee. Thus the UGC has laid down the ideal relationship in the Revised Guidelines on the Scheme of Autonomous Colleges (1998).

(iii) Mechanism for Implementation of Autonomy

An affiliated college cannot switch over to autonomous system overnight. As has been stated in the UGC guidelines there are several areas where proper preparation is necessary if college autonomy is to be implemented successfully. These are faculty preparation, departmental preparation of students and the local community. Such multi-pronged preparation shall be completed well before autonomy is sought and conferred upon a college so that no part of the college community is found unprepared for the new responsibility. For instance, seminars, workshops and consultations may be organized to make the staff familiar with the concept, objectives and rationale of autonomy. They will form part of the academic calendar of the college. In the same way, it is obligatory on the part of the departments to design suitable courses in the major and related subjects introducing new courses by changing their content, renaming obsolete courses by changing their content, updating existing courses to match the current state of art in each discipline and preparing course materials and human resources. These will be done in the light of the general objectives of autonomy and the specific objectives of the education policy.

Likewise the institution has to gear up its machinery because it has to perform many of the functions that the university has hitherto performed. It must study the academic, administrative management and financial implications of such a change to discharge its new functions efficiently.

(iv) Governance of an Autonomous College

The college will have the following committees to ensure proper management of academic, financial and general administrative affairs. Of these statutory bodies

1. The Governing Body (or Executive Committee)
2. The Academic Council
3. The Board of Studies
4. The Finance Committee occupy paramount place

The Governing Body which meets at least thricc a year shall havc powers to fix the fees and other charges payable by the students on the recommendations of the Finance Committee, institute scholarships and other prizes on the recommendations of the Academic Council and approve institution of new programmers of study leading to degrees or diplomas. It can also institute any other committees in consonance with the objectives of the autonomous college.

The Academic Council is solely responsible for all academic matters such as framing of academic policy, approval of courses, regulations, syllabi, etc. The council involves faculty at all levels and also experts from outside. The decisions taken by it will not be subject to any further rectification by the academic council or other statutory bodies of the university.

The Board of Studies is the basic constituent of the academic system of an autonomous college. Its functions will include, among other things, making rules and regulations regarding the syllabi for various courses, reviewing and updating syllabi from time to time, introducing new courses of study, determining details of continuous assessment, recommending panels of examiners under the semester system etc. It can suggest methodologies for innovative teaching and evaluation techniques and co-ordinate research, teaching extension and other academic activities. The principal convenes the meeting of the council at least once a year.

The Finance Committee advises the Governing Body and meets at least twice a year to consider (a) the budgetary estimates receivable from the UGC and non-government sources and income from fees etc., collected for the activities to undertake the scheme of autonomy and (b) audited accounts for the above.

Besides these statutory committees, the college has other committees such as the Planning and Evaluation Committee, Admission Committee, Library Committee and the Student Welfare, Co-curricular Activities Committee, Awards Committee, Appeals and Grievances Committee, Sports and Games etc. The UGC will provide assistance, payable annually to autonomous colleges to meet their additional and special needs. It can be seen that the Guidelines of the UGC are exhaustive and helpful for proper functioning of the autonomous system.

In a paper on The Performance of Autonomous Colleges, S.S. Rathi (2003) has passed strictures on autonomous system. He observed that all universities are autonomous but not necessarily good. It is, therefore, meaningless to expect the system of autonomous colleges to deliver goods. Moreover, there is danger of divisive obscurantism and fissiparous tendencies, making inroads in syllabi with some of the minority and communal groups being ardent supporters of the concept of autonomous colleges. In academic terms, the autonomous college might prove to be disastrous with each college having its own syllabi, there would be multitude of standards, each non-comparable with others. Linkage between under-graduate education, post-graduate education and research would be weakened. In the end, growth of physical, liberal and social sciences and thus, basic research would suffer, as total emphasis would be on marketable education.

In an editorial entitled, Further Empowerment of Autonomous Colleges, Raja Gopalan, S. (2003) while backing up the scheme of autonomous system, stated that the scheme should ensure comparability of the products of the autonomous colleges.

The visibility of the pronounced variations in the standards of valuation adopted by the autonomous colleges is very glaring. The substitution of grading for marking was not of much help because the grading was done only with reference to the student population within an autonomous college. Thus ascertaining the state of a student studying in an autonomous college vis-à-vis others in other autonomous colleges continues to be problematic. He further suggested that teachers who have gained doctoral degrees should be given freedom to design courses based on their doctoral work. The name of the individual teacher who designs and delivers such courses must be mentioned in the marks or grades certificate and this would impart greater professionalism to college teachers and bring out the best in them.

At the National Seminar on College Autonomy held at Chennai (2003), N.C. Chandrasekharan came down heavily on the system in his Critique of Autonomous College. The very concept of granting autonomy to 500 colleges by the Seventh Plan period has based on the UGC's policy of selective funding. Further, he stated that initially autonomy was given a high profile in Tamil Nadu and it would be interesting to know some of the teething troubles the concept met with. In one city college, autonomy was granted only for two departments to be withdrawn subsequently. In another city college, the day section was autonomous whereas the evening section was under affiliating system. To make a mockery of the syllabi, the entire university syllabus of a year was split into two halves for each subject for the two semesters. Academic councils and Board of Studies were hastily constituted. He also criticized the strange policy of 'academic apartheid' according to which students of the same class were streamed into three different class streams, the bright, the average and the below average with appropriate inoffensive nomenclature such as A, B, C. Teachers complained that bright students under-performed at the entrance level to get streamed into the below average group. It would ensure them lesser work; better grades and ultimately the degree awarded would be the same. In a way, clever students subverted the introduction of a heavier curriculum designed for excellence for a bright student easily. If the college already has a reputation, it could maintain its name irrespective of its new autonomous system. Even the university with central valuation and computerization can also ensure speedy publication of the results. Regarding the issue of discipline, he observed that discipline in autonomous colleges is not generated out of an awareness of the student but is imposed by fear of victimization from the above. The indifferent attitude of the UGC, universities and Governments has resulted in a failure of the entire experiment.

While writing a report on the two-day national seminar held at Mysore on "Quality, Autonomy", The Hindu (24-09-2004) correspondent cited J.B.G. Tilak's paper on "The Problems and Prospects of Autonomous Colleges" listed out the benefits of autonomy to the managements. They were incentive grants from the UGC, control over the staff, and scope to devise self-financing courses to enhance its revenue. The benefits to the teachers included scope for innovation in teaching, curriculum design, better evaluation of students and infrastructure. Benefits to the students included choice of credits, semester system, internal valuation and higher employability.

In an article on Autonomous Institutions, published in The Hindu, Philip G. Altbach (2005) views that academic institutions and systems have become large and complex. They need careful analysis and creative ideas. Sustained financial support with an appropriate mix of accountability and autonomy should be provided.

Amrik Singh (1-3-2005) in his article in The Tribune "No More Babysitting, Please," refers to the Kothari Commission which used the phrase "babysitting" to throw light on what colleges were doing without bothering about the intrinsic value of higher education. While talking about the fee structure in autonomous colleges he says that "if fees were to be increased, the deserving and meritorious students would have to be subsidized".

In an article entitled Reconstruction of Higher Education, brought out in The Hindu on 18-5-2005, Kundai Swami, V.C. focuses on the "real weakness of higher education" lies in the structure itself. He says that one of anachronistic practices, affiliating system must vanish from Indian soil. Autonomy must be granted to as many colleges as possible. He also lamented the peculiar and unhappy situation of substantial P.G. education in colleges that have no research whatsoever. The colleges are preparing students for examinations like tutorial colleges.

In an article, "Rural Students Take Over OU" figured in Deccan Chronicle on 21-3-2006, Mir Ayoob Alikhan laments the affiliating system whose weight caused a sag and stunted the growth of Osmania University (OU). While drawing a comparison between Osmania University and Central University (CU), Hyderabad it was felt that O.U. was saddled with 779 affiliated colleges. On the other hand C.U. had no such burden. The litany of grievances went on. Funding for science projects in O.U. is around Rs. 3 crores whereas C.U. gets a whopping Rs. 135 crores. Thus affiliating system among other causes turned out to be lethal for the university to catch up with the other famous university and the author insinuated that college autonomy is the panacea.

In an article brought out in Times of India on 26-5-2007, it was reported that general education in southern India had become more job-relevant because private autonomous colleges play a bigger role than those of northern India where a huge number of students went to college because "they had nothing else to do".

It can be seen that the above authors and investigators dealt with college autonomy cursorily covering a few areas and not descanted upon the system. In the light of globalized scenario and changed paradigms, it is ardently felt that a study on the system of autonomous colleges is of great importance. Hence, it is deemed apt to make a study on the functioning of autonomous colleges.

3

RESEARCH DESIGN

It is universally acknowledged that research design decides the fate of the research proposal and its outcome. As such, it is regarded as the heart of any research. For the present study, the following aspects have been discussed at some length as they are intrinsically related to the design of the study. Research procedure includes the operational definitions of various terms used. Selection of the sample is inclusive of the sampling techniques, the reasons for selection of a particular sampling technique and the selection of sample in accordance with the variables. Selection of tools includes the preparation of suitable tool for collection of data, description of the tool constructed and the procedure followed in administering and collecting the data required for the study.

Before going into the details of the sample, sampling techniques, variables, and tools, it is imperative and worthwhile to discuss the operational definitions of the key terms used in the study.

OPERATIONAL DEFINITIONS OF THE KEY TERMS

The operational definitions of the important terms used in the present study on 'The Analytical Study of the Functioning of Autonomous Colleges' are defined hereunder:

1. *Affiliated College:* A college, which functions under the governance of a university that legislates on courses of study and holding examinations centrally on common syllabi;
2. *Autonomous College:* College that has been conferred the special status to design their curriculum and conduct examinations within the broad framework of the parent university which has the degree awarding power;
3. *Academic Freedom:* The right of the institution to chalk out its own programmes without any restrictive interference from the university;
4. *Accreditation:* Assessment and regulation of academic standards of educational institutions by a government agency;
5. *Credit:* A quantitative measure of academic work.

VARIABLES OF THE STUDY

A variable, as the name implies, is something, which varies. Variables are the conditions or characteristics that the experimenter manipulates, controls or observes. They are indispensable for any worthwhile research for the purpose of comparison. For the present study, the following variables are considered:

1. Principals of open category autonomous college and minority category autonomous college working in the two autonomous colleges

The very composition of a minority college and its administration are relatively different than those of an aided college though both receive grants from the government. Minority colleges have been protected as part of constitutional obligation. It is incumbent on the part of the state to make a minority college stand on its feet by providing all the help needed for its growth and development. Since the government cannot meet all the demands in the field of higher education, it would help all those who fill the gap. Aided colleges thus receive monetary help. There are changes regarding rules of admission and way of functioning.

Hence, a comparison between the use of the principals belonging to a minority college and non-minority college will reveal the differences as far as the problems being confronted in the implementation of autonomy;

2. **Lecturers belonging to Arts, Commerce and Science faculties belonging to the autonomous colleges**

Since there are obvious differences among the members of various faculties, it is deemed fit to take the variables of various lecturers belonging to different faculties;

3. **Students belonging to Arts, Commerce and Science belonging to the autonomous colleges**

Since there are perceptible differences among the students of faculties, it is deemed fit to take the variables of various students pursuing different branches of learning.

The rationale for choosing the above variables is discussed hereafter. College autonomy involves administrators, teaching staff and students. It is assumed that observations to be made by principals, teachers and students belonging to arts and humanities, science and commerce are divergent. Hence all the lecturers and students belonging to the above faculties in proportion to their population have been included to find out whether there is any significant difference between the problems and suggestions given by them.

SAMPLE OF THE STUDY

After finalizing the variables of the present study, consideration was given to the entire population and saw whether the entire population can be made the subject for data collection or a particular group can be selected as representative for the study concerned. Here, the present study refers to all the principals, lecturers, and students in the autonomous colleges in A.N.U.

In any research, various methods are used for selection and drawing of samples. After a detailed study of these methods, the stratified sampling method was found to be most suitable for the present research work.

A stratified random sample is in effect a weighted combination of random sub-samples joined to give an overall sample value. Since a random sample may have, by chance, an undue proportion of one type of unit in it, it is advisable to use stratified random sampling where the entire population will be divided into smaller homogenous groups or strata, and then a sample is selected within each group. Every sampling unit is placed in one of the strata prior to the selection of the sample so that the sum of the strata is identified within the population.

When employing the method, the researcher divides his population into different strata. From each of the smaller homogenous groups falling in each stratum, he draws randomly a predetermined number of units. Thus in addition to randomness, stratification introduces a secondary element of control as means of increasing precision and representation. Ideally this would require each population member to be assigned a number, and then the sample would be selected from a table of random numbers or some other random selection. In some instances, the selection of the sample may be multi-stage process. In other words, some form of randomization may be performed in several stages of the selection until the final groupings are obtained.

A sample is a small proportion of a population selected for observation and analysis. By observing the characteristics of the sample, one can make certain inferences about the characteristics of the population from which it is drawn. After finalizing the variables of the present study, consideration was given to whether the entire population is to be made the subject for data collection or a particular group is to be selected as representative for the study concerned. Of the above two, the selection of a group as representative of the whole population was found to be more suitable and convenient. Among others, the number of principal, lecturers and students will be proportionately small and so it is possible making a detailed and intensive study. This leads to accurate and reliable results. So, the researcher for collecting data selected the sampling technique.

Contrary to some popular opinion, samples are not selected haphazardly; they are chosen in a systematic random way, so that chance or the operation of probability can be utilized.

Besides considering these factors, it is very important to think about the sample to be selected. If the sample is either too large or too small it will make the study difficult and results untenable. The size of sample for the present study was decided after considering the following factors:

1. A very large number of samples were not selected as a moderate study was planned. A smaller sample will be convenient when compared with large number of sample;
2. The size and selection of the sample are also influenced by the nature of the universe. If the universe is homogenous even a small-sized sample may yield dependable and required results. If the universe is heterogeneous, small-sized samples may not be useful;
3. The size of sample is also influenced by the size of the tools to be used. If the tools are short, then a large sample can be selected or if the tools are large, then a small sample can be selected, so that, from administrative point of view, the researcher may not be put to any unnecessary troubles. In the present study, as the tool is concerned with the problems of autonomous colleges, a very large sample was not selected;
4. The sampling method also determines the size of the sample. When random sampling method is used, the samples have to be large. On the other hand, if samples are selected through stratified random sampling method, the reliability can be achieved even with the help of the small-sized samples.

In any research, various methods are employed for selection and drawing samples. After a detailed study of all these methods the stratified random sample was found to be the most suitable method for the present research work. In the method the entire population will be divided into smaller homogeneous groups or strata to get more accurate representation. Later a sample is selected within each group.

Thus, a sample of 2 principals, 64 lecturers and 130 students belonging to the two autonomous colleges in A.N.U. was selected for the present study. After careful scrutiny a few questionnaires, which had not been properly filled in, have been omitted. The following table shows the sample distribution.

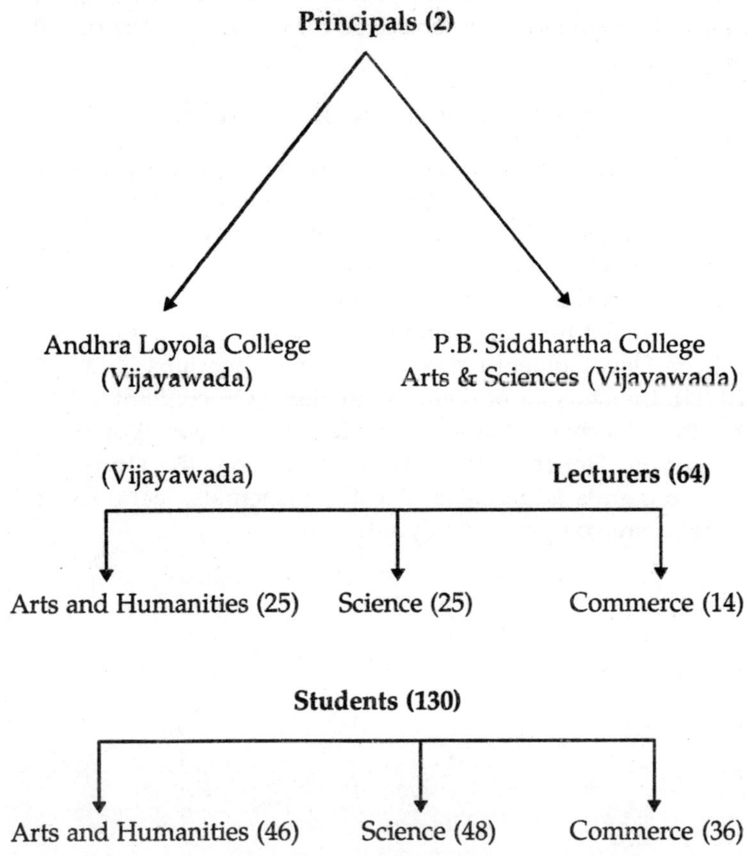

TOOL OF THE STUDY

A research tool plays a pivotal role in any worthwhile research as it is the sole factor in determining the sound data and in arriving at correct conclusions about the problem or study in hand, which ultimately helps in providing suitable remedial measures to the problem concerned for convenience's sake the questions had been converted into statement at a later stage.

Considering the merits and limitations of the selection or preparation of tools, the researcher has no other option other than constructing a tool for the present study, as there are no standardized tools on the subject. So the researcher constructed a questionnaire.

ADMINISTRATION OF THE TOOL

The questionnaire was administered on a sample of two principals, sixty five lecturers and one hundred and forty students. Some of the questionnaires have been omitted as they fail to stand the test reliability and validity. Chairpersons of various committees were also included in the sample of lecturers. The researcher, though waited for long, could not get responses from the Dean, College Development Council, Acharya Nagarjuna University (ANU), the Director of Southern Regional Office (SERO), UGC, and the Chairman of Andhra Pradesh State Council of Higher Education. Hence, they were omitted from the study. The questionnaires administered to the principals, lecturers and students are going to be analyzed.

4

ANALYSIS OF DATA

Analysis of data is of paramount importance in any research work. However valid, reliable the data may be, it does not serve any worthwhile purpose unless it is carefully edited, systematically analyzed, intelligently interpreted and rationally concluded. Hence, the next step in the process of research, after the collection of data, is the organization, analysis and interpretation of data and formulation of conclusions and generalizations to get a meaningful picture out of the raw information collected. The analysis and interpretation of data involve the objective material in the possession of the researcher and his subjective reactions derived from the data.

Analysis of data means studying the tabulate material in order to determine inherent facts for meanings. It involves breaking down the existing complex factors into simpler parts and putting the parts together in new arrangements for purposes of interpretation.

The information obtained from the principals, the lecturers and the students of the autonomous colleges was presented and analyzed hereunder. After analyzing the responses of the principals, the lecturers and the students it was intended to be befitting to juxtapose some of their responses on some crucial issues given towards the end of the chapter.

Table–4.1

PRINCIPALS' VIEWS

Regarding College Autonomy and Financial Problems (No =2)

	Statement	*Views*
1.	There is inordinate delay in the release of funds by the U.G.C.	Yes (100%) No
2.	Your college has resource crunch, which impedes its performance.	Yes No (100%)

As the Table–4.1 shows, the principals working in the autonomous colleges affiliated to Acharya Nagarjuna University agreed upon the two aspects of economic issues bearing on their colleges' performance. There was a complete consensus that there was inordinate delay in the release of funds by the UGC.

However, the principals replied that they did not have any resource crunch, which impeded their performance. What is striking is the fact that there was no difference of opinions between the principals of open-ended autonomous college and minority status-obtained autonomous college regarding the issue.

As the Table–4.2 shows, the college did not form a consortium with any autonomous college for mutual co–operation. However, they had been sharing expertise and human resources for teaching programmed from the teaching staff of the university, which helped them in designing curricula, evaluation of students. The other area in which their help was useful was their presence in the Board of Studies as advisors. There was no difference of opinions between the principals of open-ended autonomous college and minority status-obtained autonomous college.

Table–4.2
PRINCIPALS' VIEWS
Regarding Co-ordination with University Departments and Other Autonomous Colleges (No = 2)

Statement	Views
1. You have formed a consortium with an autonomous college for mutual co-operation.	Yes No (100%)
2. You have been sharing expertise and human resources for teaching programmed.	Yes (100%) No
3. You are taking help from the teaching staff of the university.	Yes (100%) No
4. Name the areas in which their help is useful.	(a) Designing the curricula (100%) (b) Evaluation of the students (50%) (c) Their presence in the Board of Studies as advisors (100%)

Table–4.3
PRINCIPALS' VIEWS
Regarding Autonomy-Pattern of Work (No = 2)

Statement	Views
1. The system of autonomy has enhanced workload for lecturers.	Yes (100%) No
2. It is necessary to evolve separate norms of workload for lecturers working in autonomous colleges.	Yes (100%) No
3. You are facing the problem of understaffing.	Yes No (100%)
4. The system of appointing lecturers on ad-hoc basis affects the functioning of autonomy.	Yes (100%) No
5. Kindly suggest any other alternative.	(a) Regular appointment of teaching staff (50%). (b) Regularization of ad-hoc lectures (50%)

As the Table–4.3 shows the system of autonomy enhanced the workload of lecturers. So the principals (100%) saw the need to evolve separate norms of workload for lectures working in autonomous colleges. They did not have the problem of understaffing. However, they expressed that appointing lecturers on ad-hoc basis affected the function of autonomous colleges. The suggestions put forward by them were regular appointment of teaching staff and regularization of ad-hoc lecturers. There was complete concurrence of views between the principals.

Table–4.4

PRINCIPALS' VIEWS

Regarding Reliability of Evaluation (No = 2)

	Statement	*Views*
1.	The students often question the reliability of internal assessment.	Yes No (100%)
2.	There is provision to improve marks obtained in internal assessment.	Yes No (100%)
3.	There are other problems in internal assessment.	Yes No (100%)
4.	If so, kindly state them.	–

As the Table-4.4 shows, the students did not question the reliability of evaluation. Similarly there was no provision to improve the marks obtained in internal assessment. The principals asserted that there were no other problems as far as internal examinations were concerned. The principals saw an eye to eye with each other on all other issues.

As the Table–4.5 shows, the courses had been restructured. However, they did not implement cafeteria or choice-based credit system. The courses had been introduced after viewing the job potential. There was provision in the courses for job experience or practical training. The syllabus was need-based. The additional papers, which had been introduced, were Mathematics, Problem-Solving Session and Communication Skills. Nevertheless, only the minority college introduced a subject on value education. But for the question of introducing value education compulsory for all students, there was no difference of views between the principals.

Table–4.5

PRINCIPALS' VIEWS

Regarding Restructuring of Courses (No = 2)

	Statement	*Views*
1.	The courses have been restructured.	Yes (100%) No
2.	You have implemented cafeteria system.	Yes No
3.	There is provision in the courses for job experience or practical training.	Yes (100%) No
4.	The syllabus is need-based.	Yes (100%) No
5.	You have introduced the courses after viewing job potential.	Yes (100%) No
6.	You have entered into any tie-ups with any industry regarding jobs.	Yes (100%) No
7.	Kindly state the additional papers introduced.	1. Mathematics and Problems Solving session and 2. Communication skills.
8.	You have introduced any subject on value education compulsory for all students.	Yes (50%) No (50%)

As the self-explanatory Table–4.6 shows, the principals opted for an autonomous (also affiliated) college for it had the inherent advantages like freedom in designing the syllabi, semester system (which could be followed as the college had freedom to go for it) incentive marks for classroom attendance and pedagogical methods and continuous internal assessment. Barring marks given to classroom attendance, the principals agreed upon all the rest of the issues.

Table–4.6
PRINCIPALS' VIEWS
Regarding Autonomous and Affiliated Colleges (No = 2)

Statement	*Views*
1. Of the two types of colleges – non–autonomous and affiliated – state your preference.	(a) Autonomous affiliated (100%) (b) Non-autonomous affiliated
2. Kindly give the reasons for your preference.	(a) Semester system (100%) (b) Freedom in designing the syllabi (100%) (c) Incentive marks for classroom attendance (50%) (d) Better evaluation and pedagogical methods can be adopted (100%) (e) Continuous internal assessment (100%)

Table–4.7
PRINCIPALS' VIEWS
Regarding Measuring Professional Competency (No = 2)

Statement	*Views*
1. You have evolved some system intended to assess the professional competency of teachers.	Yes (100%) No
2. The assessment you have chosen	(a) Periodical self-evaluation by the teachers (b) Institutional assessment of teacher's performance (c) Student evaluation of teachers' performance (d) All (100%)
3. Kindly state how it is helpful in improving academic atmosphere.	(a) Correctional measures were suggested to the staff members concerned (100%) (b) It helps in understanding the ground reality (100%) (c) Systems have a say in the system thereby making them participatory (100%).

As the Table–4.7 shows, in the autonomous colleges, a system had been evolved to assess the professional competency of teachers. It included periodical self-evaluation by the teachers, institutional assessment of teachers' performance, and students' evaluation of teachers' performance. They were helpful in improving the academic atmosphere in many ways. With the help of the assessment given, correctional measures had been suggested to the lecturers. Further, it helped in understanding the ground reality about them. Above all, students had a say in the system thereby making them participatory in the system. There was complete consensus between the principals regarding the issues.

Table–4.8

PRINCIPALS' VIEWS

Regarding Problems and Suggestions for the Success of Autonomous Colleges (No = 2)

Statement	*Views*
1. Kindly state the problems being confronted by autonomous colleges.	(a) Delay in releasing normal assistance by the UGC (100%) (b) Designing courses relevant to society is very difficult (100%) (c) University should allow us to do what we want (100%)
2. Kindly give some suggestions for the success of autonomous colleges.	(a) Foolproof examination system (100%) (b) Committed and dedicated stafff and rapport among them (100%) (c) The UGC and the state government should respect the spirit of autonomy (100%).

The Table–4.8 shows, the problems being confronted by autonomous colleges as conceived by the principals. It was held that there had been delay in releasing of normal assistance by the UGC. The other problem was that it was very difficult to design courses in consonance with the needs of society. There was absolute consensus between the principals regarding the problems.

Regarding suggestions for the success of autonomous college, all the principals maintained that foolproof examination would ensure the success of an autonomous college. Committed and dedicated staff and rapport among them, co-operation from the government and the UGC were the other important factors, which would make college autonomy a success.

Table–4.9
PRINCIPALS' VIEWS
Regarding Educational Technology (No = 2)

Statement	*Views*
1. You are making use of audio-visual aids.	Yes (100%) No
2. There is some scope for learner-centered instruction in the classroom.	Yes (100%) No
3. Kindly state the other innovative practices introduced in the teaching learning process.	1. Group discussion (100%) 2. Project work (100%) 3. Student-seminars (100%) 4. Assignment (100%)

The Table–4.9 makes it evident that the lectures were making use of audio-visual aids. Moreover, there was scope for learner-centred instruction in the classroom. They introduced many an innovative practice in the teaching and learning process. They were group discussion, project work, student seminars and assignments given to the students. There was absolute consensus pertaining to all the areas in educational technology.

The self–explanatory Table–4.10 throws light on the problems pertaining to the pattern of workload in autonomous colleges.

Cutting across the faculty lines, most of the lecturers (87%) felt that the system of autonomy had enhanced workload for lecturers. Hence they wished the necessity to evolve separate norms of workload (71%) for lecturers working in autonomous colleges. The problem of understaffing figured prominently (61%). On the other hand, a few lecturers answered in the negative regarding the increase of workload. They did not see any need to work out separate norms of workload.

Table–4.10

LECTURERS' VIEWS

Regarding Pattern of Workload (No = 64)

Statement	Lecturers in		
	Arts and Humanities	*Science*	*Commerce*
1	*2*	*3*	*4*
1. The system of autonomy has enhanced workload for lecturers.	Yes (92%) No (8%)	Yes (80%) No (20%)	Yes (90%) No (10%)
2. If so, it is necessary to evolve separate norms of workload for lecturers working in autonomous colleges.	Yes (72%) No (28%)	Yes (68%) No (38%)	Yes (71%) No (29%)
3. You are facing the problem of under-staffing.	Yes (52%) No (48%)	Yes (64%) No (36%)	Yes (66%) No (40%)
4. The system of appointing lecturers on adhoc basis affects the functioning of autonomy.	Yes (88%) No (12%)	Yes (92%) No (8%)	Yes (90%) No (10%)
5. Kindly state any other alternative.	(a) Permanent appointments with scale of pay for better performance (32%)	(a) Permanent appointments with scale of pay for better performance (36%)	(a) Permanent appointments with scale of pay for better performance (30%)

(Contd...)

1	2	3	4
	(b) Autonomous colleges should be given the freedom to select and appoint the lecturers (62%)	(b) Autonomous colleges should be given the freedom to select and appoint the lecturers (53%)	(b) Autonomous colleges should be given the freedom to select and appoint the lecturers (60%)
	(c) The salaries of such lecturers may be adequately increased (86%)	(c) The salaries of such lectures may be adequately increased (92%)	(c) The salaries of such lectures may be adequately increased (80%)
	(d) Their services may be regularized after a certain period of time even if it does not involve extending grant-in-aid to them (86%)	(d) Their services may be regularized after a certain period of time even if it does not involve extending grant-in-aid to them (92%)	(d) Their services may be regularized after a certain period of time even if it does not involve extending grant-in-aid to them (80%)

In a similar view most of the lecturers (90%) opined that appointment of lecturers on ad-hoc bases effected the functioning of the autonomous college. They put forward various views when they were asked to suggest any other alternative. Their responses encompassed similar lines either to put an end to the obnoxious practice or to alleviate it by making some reforms into it. Permanent appointments, the freedom to be given to autonomous colleges to appoint their teaching staff, the rise of salaries of such lecturers and regularizing their services after a span of some period were the reforms. The views thus expressed by Arts, Science and Commerce lecturers; one can find a great degree of similarity.

As per the Table–4.11 (*See on next page*), both the colleges were following semester system. Most of the lecturers said that the reliability of internal assessment was not often questioned. Though they were a few lecturers who said that the assessment was often questioned, it was very marginal. There was no provision to improve the marks obtained in internal assessment in both the colleges. However, there were a whopping percentage of lecturers who identified the problems with the evaluation. Many teachers said that they were wanting in knowledge regarding scientific test-construction. Even the evaluation had been done perfunctorily since each teacher was burdened with a large number of answer scripts. Sometimes, students knew the question papers sought to assess internal assessment but this recrimination was marginal and was heard from the lecturers belonging to the faculties of Arts, Science and Commerce. Some lecturers felt that evaluation should be more objective. According to some, objective type questions should be increased to make evaluation more objective. Thus there was no significant divergence of views among the lecturers belonging to Arts, Science and Commerce regarding reliability of evaluation.

Table–4.11

LECTURERS' VIEWS

Regarding Reliability of Evaluation (No = 64)

Statement	*Lecturers in*		
	Arts and Humanities	*Science*	*Commerce*
1	2	3	4
1. You are following semester system.	Yes (100%) No (0%)	Yes (100%) No (0%)	Yes (100%) No (0%)
2. The reliability of internal assessment often questioned by the students.	Yes (8%) No (92%)	Yes (12%) No (88%)	Yes (6%) No (94%)
3. There is provision to improve the marks obtained in internal assessment.	Yes (0%) No (100%)	Yes (0%) No (100%)	Yes (0%) No (100%)
4. There are other problems with the evaluation.	Yes (36%) No (64%)	Yes (48%) No (52%)	Yes (41%) No (59%)
5. If so, specify them.	(a) Teachers are not adequately trained in test construction and so the testing is by and large unsatisfactory (26%)	(a) Teachers are not adequately trained in test construction and so the testing is by and large unsatisfactory (44%)	(a) Teachers are not adequately trained in test construction and so the testing is by and large unsatisfactory (20%)

(Contd...)

1	2	3	4
	(b) Evaluation (marking) has been done perfunctorily since each teacher is burdened with a large number of answer scripts (24%)	(b) Evaluation (marking) has been done perfunctorily since each teacher is burdened with a large number of answer scripts (44%)	(b) Evaluation (marking has been) done perfunctorily since each teacher is burdened with a large number of answer scripts (20%)
	(c) Need to increased more objectivity in evaluation (20%)	(c) Need to increase more objectivity in evaluation (52%)	(c) Evaluation should be more objective (30%)
	(d) Sometimes question papers are known to the students before the exams (16%)	(d) Difference between internal and external marks is to be narrowed down (20%)	(d) Students should be evaluated only academically without taking attendance into consideration (30%).
	(e) Students should be evaluated only academically without taking attendance into consideration (16%)	(e) Students should be evaluated only academically without taking attendance into consideration (16%)	(e) Objective type questions are to be introduced to make evaluation more objective (20%)
	(f) Objective type questions are to be introduced to make evaluation more objective and unbiased (28%)	(f) Objective type questions are to be introduced to make evaluation more objective (20%)	

Table–4.12

LECTURERS' VIEWS

Regarding Co–ordination with University Departments and Autonomous Colleges (No = 64)

Statement	*Lecturers in*		
	Arts and Humanities	*Science*	*Commerce*
1	*2*	*3*	*4*
1. You have formed a consortium with autonomous colleges for mutual co-operation.	Yes (0%) No (100%)	Yes (0%) No (100%)	Yes (0%) No (100%)
2. If so, name the college	–	–	–
3. You have been sharing expertise and human resource for teaching programmes	Yes (48%) No (52%)	Yes (76%) No (24%)	Yes (50%) No (50%)
4. You are taking help from the teaching staff of the university	Yes (100%) No (0%)	Yes (100%) No (0%)	Yes (100%) No (0%)

(Contd...)

1	2	3	4
5. If so, state the areas in which their help is useful	(a) Their presence in the Board of Studies as advisors It is mandatory (72%) (b) Designing the curriculum (in framing the semester syllabi) (76%) (c) In designing the pattern of the question paper (28%) (d) In conducting seminars for the academic staff and students (20%) (e) Visiting the college in the capacity of guest lecturers (22%)	(a) Their presence in the Board of Studies as advisors It is mandatory (76%) (b) Designing the curriculum (in framing the semester syllabi (68%) (c) In designing the pattern of the question paper (24%) (d) In conducting seminars for the academic staff and students (12%) (e) Visiting the college in the capacity of guest lecturers (12%)	(a) Their presence in the Board of Studies as advisors It is mandatory (70%) (b) Designing the curriculum (in framing the semester syllabi) (70%) (c) In designing the pattern of the question paper (30%) (d) In conducting seminars for the academic staff and students (20%) (e) Visiting the college in the capacity of guest lecturers (30%)

The Table–4.12 shows that the colleges did not forge a consortium with any other autonomous college. However, they had been sharing expertise and human resources for teaching programmes (58%).

All the lecturers of Arts, Commerce and Science held that they were taking help from the teaching staff of the university in many ways (100%). The teaching staff was present in the Board of Studies. They also helped in designing the curricula, framing the semester syllabi and in designing the pattern of the question papers. Further, they sought help from the teaching staff of the university in matters of conducting seminars for staff and students. They also called on the college to give guest lecturers.

This sharing of expertise and human resource was conspicuous to all the subjects. It can be seen that all the lecturers voiced the same views.

The autonomous colleges under the jurisdiction of Acharya Nagarjuna University did not implement choice-based credit system. According to most of the lecturers belonging to Arts, Science and Commerce, credit system had many advantages (73%). The lecturers have cited the advantages of the system. There would be more flexibility in opting courses (13%). The diversification would enable students to face competitive examinations (23%). Arts students could learn science subjects vice versa in consonance with their interests (17%).

Most of the lecturers (93%) felt that they had been taken into confidence while taking decision that affect their class-work and had been given freedom to plan syllabi. Barring a few instances lecturers belonging to Arts, Sciences and Commerce expressed the same views.

As was evidenced in the Table–4.14 (*See on page* 53), the lecturers belonging to Arts, Science and Commerce considered that autonomous system was better than affiliated system. They adduced several reasons for their preference. In autonomous colleges, lecturers had freedom in designing the curriculum and the evaluation pattern (65%).

Table–4.13

LECTURERS' VIEWS

Regarding Restructuring of Syllabus (No = 64)

Statement	*Lecturers in*		
	Arts and Humanities	*Science*	*Commerce*
1	*2*	*3*	*4*
1. The credit system has been implemented in your college.	Yes (0%) No (100%)	Yes (0%) No (100%)	Yes (0%) No (100%)
2. Mention the advantages of the credit system.	(a) Academic flexibility (72%)	(a) Academic flexibility (72%)	(a) Academic flexibility (70%)
	(b) Diversification of courses (11%)	(b) Diversification of courses (12%)	(c) Diversification of courses (20%)
	(c) Flexibility in opting courses (16%)	(c) Flexibility in opting courses (12%)	(c) Flexibility in opting courses (10%)
	(d) Better ability to face competitive and other exams (28%)	(d) Better ability to face competitive and other exams (20%)	(d) Better ability to face competitive and other exams (20%)
	(e) Arts students can learn science subjects and vice versa (16%)	(e) Scope for studying Arts and other subjects (17%)	(e) Arts students can learn science subjects and vice versa (20%)

(Contd...)

1	2	3	4
3. You have identified any problem with the credit system.	Yes (28%) No (72%)	Yes (24%) No (76%)	Yes (30%) No (70%)
4. You have been given freedom to plan your syllabus.	Yes (88%) No (12%)	Yes (92%) No (8%)	Yes (90%) No (10%)
5. You are taken into confidence when taking decisions that affect your class work.	Yes (92%) No (8%)	Yes (92%) No (8%)	Yes (90%) No (10%)

Table–4.14

LECTURERS' VIEWS

Regarding Autonomous and Affiliated Systems (No = 64)

Statement	*Lecturers in*		
	Arts and Humanities	*Science*	*Commerce*
1	2	3	*4*
1. Of the two types of colleges—autonomous and affiliated the one you consider better.	Affiliated (0%) Autonomous (100%)	Affiliated (0%) Autonomous (100%)	Affiliated (0%) Autonomous (100%)
2. Kindly give the reasons for your preference.	(a) Academic freedom in designing the curriculum and the evaluation pattern (60%) (b) Greater accountability (48%) (c) Better scope for teacher-student interaction (44%) (d) Syllabi can be completed (36%)	(a) Academic freedom in designing the curriculum and the evaluation pattern (64%) (b) Greater accountability (52%) (c) Better scope for teacher-student interaction (36%) (d) Syllabi can be completed (28%)	(a) Academic freedom in designing the curriculum and the evaluation pattern (70%) (b) Greater accountability (40%) (c) Better scope for teacher-student interaction (50%) (d) Syllabi can be completed (30%)

(Contd...)

1	2	3	4
	(e) Students gain much knowledge than those in the affiliated college (24%)	(e) Students gain much knowledge than those in the affiliated colleges (20%)	(e) Students gain much knowledge than those in the affiliated colleges (10%)
	(f) The system is flexible and gives room for changes (16%)	(f) Students are free to prepare for the exams in their own way (8%)	(f) Students are free to prepare for the exams in their own way (20%)
	(g) Students are free to prepare for the exams at their own pace (12%)	(g) Semester system practised here is better than year-end examinations (72%)	(g) Improvement of discipline among the students (70%)
	(h) Improvement of discipline among the students (56%)	(h) Examinations are conducted in time and the results are declared in time (12%)	(h) Semester system practised here is better than year-end examinations (40%).
	(i) Semester system practised here is better than year-end examinations (68%)	(i) Immediate reddressal of grievances (12%)	(i) Examinations are conducted in time and results are declared in time (10%).

(Contd...)

1	2	3	4
	(j) Examinations are conducted in time and results are declared in time (20%)	(j) Students' pattern of work is evenly spreads over the period of their study (8%)	(j) Immediate reddressal of of grievances (10%)
	(k) Immediate redressal of grievances (28%)	(k) We are getting more number of hours so that we can teach every bit of the syllabus (20%).	(k) Students' pattern of work is evenly spreads over the period of their study (10%).
	(l) Students' pattern of work is evenly spread over the period of their study (12%).	(l) New teaching techniques can be adopted (12%)	(l) Students' attendance has been improved tremendously (50%).
	(m) Students' attendance has been improved tremendously (56%)		(m) We are getting more number of hours so that we can teach every bit of the syllabus (30%).
	(n) We are getting more number of hours so that we can teach every bit of the syllabus (28%).		(n) New teaching techniques can be adopted (10%).
	(o) New teaching techniques can be adopted (8%).		

Accountability was fixed and so there was better scope for teacher-student interaction (47%). Syllabi could be completed within time. Students gained much knowledge than their counterparts in autonomous colleges. When it comes to discipline, there was considerable improvement of discipline in Arts and Commerce sections. They attended classes regularly. The semester system followed in autonomous colleges was better than year-end examinations in affiliated colleges. Results could be announced within time. New teaching techniques could be adopted. Grievances were redressed at once. Arts and Humanities, Commerce lecturers' suggestions were more compared to the suggestions of Science lecturers.

As the Table–4.15 (*See on next page*) shows, the colleges evolved the system to measure professional competency of teachers (100%). The system includes periodical self-evaluation by the teachers, institutional evaluation of teachers' performance, and students' evaluation of lecturer's performance. All the lecturers felt that they were helpful in many ways in improving the academic atmosphere. First, it gave the teacher the much-needed feedback upon his own performance. It helped the teacher understand himself. Management could suggest some concrete correctional measures. Further it helped the lecturer know the ground reality about him. Lecturers were eager to introduce more innovative techniques of teaching. Though some students did not know how to evaluate their teachers, lecturers generally agreed upon the point that it helped them have a peep into the minds of students and their needs. Only some science lecturers opined that students did not know how to evaluate their lecturers.

Table–4.15

LECTURERS' VIEWS

Regarding Professional Competency (No = 64)

Statement	*Lectures in*		
	Arts & Humanities	*Science*	*Commerce*
1	*2*	*3*	*4*
1. You have evolved any system intended to assess the professional competency of teachers.	Yes (100%) No (0%)	Yes (100%) No (0%)	Yes (100%) No (0%)
2. Kindly state how it is measured:	Yes (100%) No (0%)	Yes (100%) No (0%)	Yes (100%) No (0%)
a. Periodical self-evaluation by the teachers			
b. Institutional assessment of teachers' performance.			
c. Student evaluation of teachers' performance.			
d. All			
e. None.			

(Contd...)

1	2	3	4
3. Kindly state how it is helpful in improving academic atmosphere.	(a) It gives the teachers the much-needed feedback on performance (68%)	(a) It gives the teachers the much-needed feedback on performance (50%)	(a) It gives the teachers the much-needed feedback on performance (70%)
	(b) Taken in right spirit, it helps the teacher correct himself thereby improving the academic atmosphere (64%)	(b) Taken in right spirit, it helps the teacher correct himself thereby improving the academic atmosphere (56%)	(b) Taken in right spirit it helps the teacher correct himself thereby improving the academic atmosphere (30%)
	(c) Correctional measures have been suggested to the members of the staff (68%)	(c) Correctional measures have been suggested to the members of the staff (56%)	(c) Correctional measures have been suggested to the members of the staff (30%)
	(d) It helps us know the ground reality about one self (24%)	(d) It gives a constant feedback on the areas where he needs improvement (24%)	(d) It helps us know the ground reality about ourselves (20%)
	(e) It gives a constant feedback on the areas where he needs improvement (28%)	(e) More innovative techniques of teaching are the outcome of it (8%)	(e) It gives a constant feedback on the areas where he needs improvement (30%)

(Contd...)

1	2	3	4
	(f) More innovative techniques of teaching are the outcome of it. (12%) (g) It helps us have a peep into the minds of students and their needs (16%) (h) So me of the students do not know evaluating their teachers (32%)	(f) It helps us have a peep into the minds of students and their needs (20%) (g) So me of the students do not know evaluating their teachers (28%)	(f) More innovative techniques of teaching are the outcome of it. (30%) (g) It helps us have a peep into the minds of students and their needs (10%)

Table–4.16

LECTURERS' VIEWS

Regarding Educational Technology (No = 64)

Statement	*Lectures in*		
	Arts & Humanities	*Science*	*Commerce*
1	2	3	4
1. You are using audio-visual aids in the classroom.	Yes (60%) No (40%)	Yes (96%) No (4%)	Yes (50%) No (50%)
2. There is some scope for learner-centered instruction in the classroom.	Yes (72%) No (28%)	Yes (96%) No (4%)	Yes (60%) No (40%)
3. The other innovative practices introduced in the teaching and learning process.	(a) Seminars (100%) (b) Self-study in some subjects (60%) (c) Assignments to students (100%) (d) Group discussions (96%)	(a) Seminars (100%) (b) Study-study in some subjects (40%) (c) Project work (20%) (d) Assignments to students (100%)	(a) Seminars (100%) (b) Self-study in some subjects (64%) (c) Project work (22%) (d) Assignments to students (100%)

(Contd...)

1	2	3	4
	(e) Field trips (20%)	(e) Group discussions (72%)	(e) Group discussions (96%)
	(f) Continuous internal assessment (100%)	(f) Field trips (28%)	(f) Field trips (20%)
	(g) Production of instructional material by the members of (English) department (24%)	(g) Continuous internal assessment (100%)	(g) Continuous internal assessment (100%)
	(h) Problem solving sessions (50%)	(h) Workshops (80%)	(h) Industrial visits
		(i) Problem solving sessions (48%)	(i) Workshops (10%)
			(j) Management games (20%)
			(k) Problem solving sessions (52%)

The Table–4.16 shows that Arts and Commerce lecturers were using audio-visual aids moderately. Science lecturers were availing them to the maximum possible extent (96%). According to many lecturers in Arts & Science disciplines, there was scope for learner-centered instruction in the classroom. However, almost all the science lecturers (96%) felt that there was scope for learner-centered instruction. There were many innovative teaching practices introduced by lecturers belonging to Arts, Humanities, Science and Commerce. They were, to mention a few, seminars, (100%) self-study (51%), group discussions (84%), workshops, production of instructional material protect work, management games etc. It can be seen that any lecturer did not exploit the computer technology and the other aids related to it.

The self-explanatory Table–4.17 (*See on next page*) explains the problems of autonomous colleges from the view of lecturers. Irrespective of their faculties, all the lecturers expressed more or less the same views pertaining to the problems of autonomous colleges. They are: indifference of the university and the state government (56%); absence of networking of autonomous colleges (36%); Some Universities would not like to take into consideration the marks obtained in internal assessment (76%). Some other problems listed were: too much work-load (68%); inadequacy of academic staff (12%); academic staff being not properly trained in syllabus design, teaching, methodology and testing (56%). If lecturers become inactive and uncommitted to the academic work autonomy will collapse (35%). If the lecturers do not upgrade their knowledge, system fails (28%). Ad-hoc teaching staff problems need to be addressed (52%). Co–curricular activities had not been given their due share (15%). Autonomy to P.G. courses should be granted (46%). There is lack of research activity (32%). The system curtailed students' freedom (28%). Students became more passive participants (32%). There was no divergence of views among lecturers belonging to the faculties.

Table–4.17

LECTURERS' VIEWS

Regarding Problems of Autonomous Colleges (No = 64)

Statement	*Lecturers in*		
	Arts and Humanities	*Science*	*Commerce*
1	2	3	*4*
1. Kindly list out the problems of autonomous colleges.	(a) Indifference of the university and the state government (56%) (b) Absence of networking of autonomous colleges (36%) (c) Some universities would not like to take into consideration the marks obtained in internal assessment (76%)	(a) Indifference of the university and the state government (64%) (b) Absence of networking of autonomous colleges (24%) (c) Some universities would not like to take into consideration the marks obtained in internal assessment (64%)	(a) Indifference of the university and the state government (60%) (b) Absence of networking of autonomous colleges (21%) (c) Some universities would not like to take into consideration the marks obtained in internal assessment (70%)

(Contd...)

1	2	3	4
	(d) Too much workload (68%)	(d) Too much workload (64%)	(d) Too much workload (60%)
	(e) Inadequacy of academic staff (12%)	(e) Inadequacy of academic staff (20%)	(e) Inadequacy of academic staff (10%)
	(f) Academic staff not properly trained in syllabus design, teaching, methodology and testing (56%)	(f) Academic staff not properly trained in syllabus design, teaching, methodology and testing (48%)	(f) Academic staff not properly trained in syllabus design, teaching, methodology and testing (40%)
	(g) If lecturers become inactive and uncommitted to the academic work, autonomy will collapse (35%)	(g) If lecturers become inactive and uncommitted to the academic work, autonomy will collapse (7) (28%)	(g) If lecturers become inactive and uncommitted to the academic work, autonomy will collapse (3) (30%)
	(h) If the lecturers do not upgrade their knowledge, systems fails (28%)	(h) If the lecturers do not upgrade their knowledge, systems fails (24%)	(h) If the lecturers do not upgrade their knowledge, systems fails (30%)

(Contd...)

1	2	3	4
	(i) Ad-hoc teaching staff's problems need to be addressed (52%) (j) Co-curricular activities have not be given their due share (15%) (k) Autonomy to P.G. courses should be granted (46%) (l) Lack of research activity (32%) (m) The system curtails students' freedom (28%) (n) Students become more passive participants (32%)	(i) Ad-hoc teaching staff's problems need to be addressed (48%) (j) Co-curricular activities have not be given their due share (12%) (k) Autonomy to P.G. courses should be granted (44%) (l) Lack of research activity (36%) (m) The system curtails students' freedom (8%) (n) Students become more passive participants (28%)	(i) Ad-hoc teaching staff's problems need to be addressed (50%) (j) Co-curricular activities have not be given their due share (10%) (k) Autonomy to P.G. courses should be granted (30%) (l) Lack of research activity (40%) (m) The system curtails students' freedom (40%) (n) Students become more passive participants (20%)

Table–4.18

LECTURERS' VIEWS

Regarding Suggestions for the Success of Autonomous Colleges (No = 64)

Statement	*Lecturers in*		
	Arts & Humanities	*Science*	*Commerce*
1	2	3	4
(a) Kindly give suggestions for the success of autonomous colleges.	(a) Complete autonomy should be granted in academic matters i.e. starting of new courses, restructuring of existing courses based on need and opportunities available (94%). (b) Semester system should be implemented (70%). (c) Ratio of internal should not exceed (56%). (d) Co-operation between government, autonomous colleges and the U.G.C. (38%)	(a) Complete autonomy should be granted in academic matters i.e. starting of new courses, restructuring of existing courses based on need and opportunities available (94%). (b) Semester system should be implemented (72%). (c) Ratio of internal should not exceed (50%). (d) Co-operation between government, autonomous colleges and the U.G.C. (42%)	(a) Complete autonomy should be granted in academic matters i.e. starting of new courses, restructuring of existing courses based on need and opportunities available (98%). (b) Semester system should be implemented (74%). (c) Ratio of internal should not exceed (44%). (d) Co-operation between government, autonomous colleges and the U.G.C. (44%).

(Contd...)

1	2	3	4
	(e) Absolute freedom has to be given to departments to structure and restructure syllabi (20%). (f) Proper planning (48%). (g) The workload of teachers may be reduced in order to enable them to introduce innovations like projects, surveys and fieldwork as part of the curriculum and supervise them effectively (80%). (h) Teachers of autonomous colleges should be properly trained in syllabus design teaching methodology and testing (72%). (i) There could be refresher courses exclusively for teachers in autonomous colleges (28%).	(e) Absolute freedom has to be given to departments to structure and restructure syllabi (24%) (f) Proper planning (40%) (g) The workload of teachers may be reduced in order to enable them to introduce innovations like projects, surveys and fieldwork as part of the curriculum and supervise them effectively (70%). (h) Teachers of autonomous colleges should be properly trained in syllabus design teaching methodology and testing (64%). (i) There could be refresher courses exclusively for teachers in autonomous colleges (26%).	(e) Absolute freedom has to be given to departments to structure and restructure syllabi (16%). (f) Proper planning (56%). (g) The workload of teachers may be reduced in order to enable them to introduce innovations like projects, surveys and fieldwork as part of the curriculum and supervise them effectively (90%). (h) Teachers of autonomous colleges should be properly trained in syllabus design teaching methodology and testing (80%). (i) There could be refresher courses exclusively for teachers in autonomous colleges (30%).

(Contd...)

1	2	3	4
	(j) The U.G.C. may organize curriculum development renewal programmers for autonomous colleges with suitable resource persons (32%). (k) Academic staff colleges should come forward to orient teachers in new areas (28%). (l) Service conditions of the lecturers appointed on the ad-hoc basis should be improved (18%). (m) Examinations must be conducted fool proof (60%). (n) Co-operation between the staff and management and understanding between students and staff (68%).	(j) The U.G.C. may organize curriculum development renewal programmes for autonomous colleges with suitable resource persons (36%) (k) Academic staff colleges should come forward to orient teachers in new areas (38%). (l) Service conditions of the lecturers appointed on the ad-hoc basis should be improved (18%). (m) Examinations must be conducted foolproof (80%). (n) Co-operation between the staff and management and understanding between students and staff (66%).	(j) The U.G.C. may organize curriculum development renewal programmes for autonomous colleges with suitable resource persons (40%). (k) Academic staff colleges should come forward to orient teachers in new areas (18%). (l) Service conditions of the lecturers appointed on the ad-hoc basis should be improved (18%). (m) Examinations must be conducted fool proof (76%). (n) Co-operation between the staff and management and understanding between students and staff (70%).

(Contd...)

1	2	3	4
	(o) More extension activities that will involve the students and the neighborhood are necessary (28%). (p) Encouragement to teachers who introduce innovative teaching practices (34%). (q) Industry-college interaction and as per the need, syllabi should be up-dated (22%). (r) Support for meaningful research (11%). (s) Job-oriented courses should be introduced (22%).	(o) More extension activities that will involve the students and the neighbourhood are necessary (36%). (p) Encouragement to teachers who introduce innovative teaching practices (30%). (q) Industry-college interaction and as per the need, syllabi should be up-dated (22%). (r) Support for meaningful research (9%) (s) Job-oriented courses should be introduced (28%).	(o) More extension activities that will involve the students and the neighbourhood are necessary (32%). (p) Encouragement to teachers who introduce innovative teaching practices (32%). (q) Industry-college interaction and as per the need, syllabi should be up-dated (16%). (r) Support for meaningful research (13%). (s) Job-oriented courses should be introduced (25%)

As the Table–4.18 shows, most of the students voiced the same views with regard to the measures, which would ensure the success of college autonomy. They are mentioned hereafter. Complete autonomy should be granted in academic matters i.e. starting of new courses, restructuring of existing courses based on need and opportunities available. Semester system should be implemented. Ratio of internal should not exceed after certain limit. There should be fruitful co-operation between government, autonomous colleges and the U.G.C. Absolute freedom had to be given to departments to structure and restructure syllabi. Proper planning should be there (48%).

The workload of teachers may be reduced in order to enable them to introduce innovations like projects, surveys and fieldwork as part of the curriculum and supervise them effectively. Teachers of Autonomous colleges should be properly trained in syllabus design, teaching methodology and testing. There could be refresher courses exclusively for teachers in autonomous colleges. The UGC may organize curriculum development renewal programmes for autonomous colleges with suitable resource persons.

It was felt that Academic Staff Colleges should come forward to orient teachers in new areas. Service conditions of the lecturers appointed on the ad-hoc basis should be ameliorated. Examinations must be conducted pool-proof. There should be meaningful co-operation between the staff and management and understanding between students and staff. More extension activities that would involve the students and the neighbourhood were necessary. Encouragement should be given to teachers who introduced innovative teaching practices. Industry-college interaction and as per the need, syllabi should be up-dated. There should be support for meaningful research. Job–oriented courses should be introduced. Cutting across all the disciplines, lecturers voiced the same views though there was some mild degree of differences with regard to the percentage.

Table–4.19

STUDENTS' VIEWS

Regarding Reliability of Internal Assessment (No = 130)

Statements	*Students*		
	Arts & Humanities	*Science*	*Commerce*
1	2	3	4
1. The Internal Assessment is unbiased.	Yes (88%) No (12%)	Yes (84%) No (16%)	Yes (92%) No (8%)
2. You have identified some other problems regarding evaluation.	Yes (84%) No (16%)	Yes (90%) No (10%)	Yes (65%) No (35%)
3. If so, name them.	(a) The average marks of the two internals have been given but it is good if they take the better of the two into consideration (20%). (b) Valuation of the scripts should be fair and perfect (24%).	(a) The average marks of the two internals have been given but it is good if they take the better of the two into consideration (18%). (b) Valuation of the scripts should be fair and perfect (23%).	(a) The average marks of the two internals have been given but it is good if they take the better of the two into consideration (15%). (b) Valuation of the scripts should be fair and perfect (10%).

(Contd...)

1	2	3	4
	(c) Only one mid exam should be conducted. Seminars and assignments should be given adequate weightage (32%). (d) It is difficult for N.C.C. and N.S.S. students to get permission to attend camps (2%). (e) Percentage of marks in the final exam comes down as the internal marks are added to it (12%). (f) Syllabi have been completed in a slipshod manner (22%). (g) Students are overburdened with examinations (21%). (h) Students are goaded to do endless variety of work (20%).	(c) Only one mid exam should be conducted. Seminars and assignments should be given adequate weightage (30%). (d) It is difficult for N.C.C. and N.S.S. students to get permission to attend camps (2%). (e) Percentage of marks in the final exam comes down as the internal marks are added to it (12%). (f) Syllabi have been completed in a slipshod manner (21%). (g) Students are overburdened with examinations (20%). (h) Students are goaded to do endless variety of work (17%).	(c) Only one mid exam should be conducted. Seminars and assignments should be given adequate weightage (15%). (d) It is difficult for N.C.C. and N.S.S. students to get permission to attend camps (1%). (e) Percentage of marks in the final exam comes down as the internal marks are added to it (15%). (f) Syllabi have been completed in a slipshod manner (10%). (g) Students are overburdened with examinations (18%). (h) Students are goaded to do endless variety of work (6%).

(Contd...)

1	2	3	4
	(i) Students have little time to look after anything besides examinations (32%). (j) We have little time to play (26%).	(i) Students have little time to look after anything besides examinations (30%). (j) We have little time to play (24%).	(i) Students have little time to look after any thing besides examinations (10%). (j) We have little time to play (10%).

The above self-explanatory Table–4.19 explains reliability of internal assessment from students' point of view.

Most of the Arts and Humanities students felt that the internal assessment was unbiased (88%). However, they identified other problems regarding evaluation with a little degree of differences. They are given hereunder: They felt that the average marks of the two internals had been given but it was good if they took the better of the two into consideration (20%). Valuation of the scripts should be fair and perfect (24%). Only one mid exam should be conducted. Seminars and assignments should be given adequate weightage (32%). It was difficult for N.C.C. and N.S.S. students to get permission to attend camps (2%). Percentage of marks in the final exam came down as the internal marks were added to it (12%). Syllabi had been completed in a slipshod manner (22%). Students were overburdened with examinations (21%). Students were goaded to do endless variety of work (20%). Students had little time to look after anything besides examinations (32%) and they had little time to play (26%).

Most Science students felt that the internal assessment was unbiased (84%). However, they identified other problems regarding evaluation listed out hereafter. They are: The average marks of the two internals had been given but it is good if they take the better of the two into consideration (18%). Valuation of the scripts should be fair and perfect (23%). Only one mid exam should be conducted. Seminars and assignments should be given adequate weightage (30%). It was difficult for N.C.C. and N.S.S. students to get permission to attend camps (2%). Percentage of marks in the final exam came down as the internal marks were added to it (12%). Syllabi had been completed in a slipshod manner (21%). Students were overburdened with examinations (20%). Students were goaded to do endless variety of work (17%). Students had little time to look after anything besides examinations (30%) and they had little time to play (24%).

Most of the Commerce students felt that the internal assessment was unbiased (92%). However, they identified other problems regarding evaluation. They are given hereafter: The average marks of the two internals had been given but it is good if they take the better of the two into consideration (15%). Valuation of the scripts should be fair and perfect (10%). Only one mid exam should be conducted. Seminars and assignments should be given adequate weightage (15%). It was difficult for N.C.C. and N.S.S. students to get permission to attend camps (1%). Percentage of marks in the final exam came down as the internal marks were added to it (15%). Syllabi had been completed in a slipshod manner (10%). Students were overburdened with examinations (18%). Students were goaded to do endless variety of work (6%). Students had little time to look after anything besides examinations (10%) and they were of the opinion that they had little time to play (10%).

As the Table–4.20 shows, (*See on next page*) the percentage of students, who felt that the syllabus was burden, some was marginal (about 28%). About 70 per cent of the students felt that the syllabus was not burdensome as the year's work was evenly divided. Regarding syllabus, most of the students opined that it was easy on account of the division of a year's work in two halves. It was only a few students who remarked that the syllabus allotted to internals was enormous as a result of which private classes were conducted to cover the syllabus. Some Commerce students saw the need to make changes in the syllabus in consonance with the recent developments.

The Table–4.21 (*See on page 77*) shows that almost all the students— Arts, Science and Commerce—showed their preference for autonomous college (99%). They adduced many reasons for their preference. They observed that autonomous college students conducted themselves in a disciplined manner (12%). Students were more prone to hard work (7%). Classes were being conducted regularly (11%). One could secure good marks. They could conduct in a responsible manner (5%). They regularly attended classes (8%). Syllabi could be designed by autonomous colleges themselves. It gives scope for assignments and internals (8%). Labs were well maintained (22%). Syllabi had been covered entirely (8%). They did not have any fear to face examinations (11%) and semester examinations were better than year-end examinations (21%). There was a moderate degree of difference as far as percentage is concerned among the students belonging to the three disciplines.

Table–4.20

STUDENTS' VIEWS

Regarding Syllabus (No = 130)

	Statement	*Students in*		
		Arts & Humanities	*Science*	*Commerce*
	1	2	3	4
1.	Syllabus is burdensome.	Yes (29%) No (71%)	Yes (25%) No (75%)	Yes (32%) No (68%)
2.	If so, comment on the syllabus.	(a) As the year's work is divided into two halves, it is easy to go through it (44 %). (b) It is very easy and limited (20%).	a. Syllabus allotted to internals is enormous. (13%). b. As a result separate private classes have been conducted to cover the syllabus (12%). c. Syllabus is limited and less compared to university syllabus (36%).	(a) It is easy because of internals (9%). (b) It should be changed according to the changing times (2%). (c) As the syllabus is limited it is easy to prepare for examinations (4%). (d) It is good (4%)

Table–4.21

STUDENTS' VIEWS

Regarding Autonomous vs. Affiliated Colleges

Statement	Students in		
	Arts & Humanities	*Science*	*Commerce*
1	*2*	*3*	*4*
1. The better of the two– an Autonomous affiliated college, or a Non-autonomous affiliated college.	Autonomous (98 %) Affiliated (2%)	Autonomous (99%) Affiliated. (1%)	Autonomous (100%) Affiliated (Nil)
2. Give the reasons for your preference.	(a) In an autonomous college students conduct themselves in a disciplined manner (14%). (b) Students are more prone to hard work (4%). (c) End semester examinations are better than year-end examinations (28%).	(a) End-semester examinations are better than year-end examinations (24%). (b) Students do not have any fear of examinations (6%). (c) Classes are being conducted regularly (4%).	(a) In an autonomous college students conduct themselves in a disciplined manner (22%). (b) Students are more prone to hard work (17%). (c) End semester examinations are better than year-end examinations (10%).

(Contd...)

1	2	3	4
	(d) Students do not have any fear of examinations (16%). (e) Classes are being conducted regularly (18%). (f) Good interaction between the teacher and the students (16%). (g) One can secure good marks (4%). (h) We can conduct ourselves in responsible manner (4%). (i) Syllabus is covered entirely (6%). (j) Regular attendance to classes (16%). (k) Syllabi can be designed by teachers (14%). (l) It gives scope for assignments and internals (6%).	(d) Good interaction between the teacher and the students (4%). (e) The syllabus has been covered entirely (4%). (f) Syllabi can be designed by teachers (6%). (g) It gives scope for assignments and internals (4%). (h) Labs are well maintained here (22%).	(d) Students do not have any fear of examinations (10%). (e) Classes are being conducted regularly (10%). (f) Good interaction between the teacher and the students (15%). (g) One can secure good marks (10%). (h) We can conduct ourselves in responsible manner (10%). (i) Syllabus is covered entirely (15%). (j) Regular attendance to classes (10%). (k) Syllabi can be designed by teachers (10%). (l) It gives scope for assignments and internals (10%).

Table–4.22

STUDENTS' VIEWS

Regarding Educational Technology (No = 130)

Statements	*Students in*		
	Arts & Humanities	*Science*	*Commerce*
1. Audio-visual aids used in the classroom.	(a) Maps (24%) (b) Projector (8%) (c) Charts (6%)	(a) Slides (13%) (b) Projector (6%) (c) Charts (8%)	(a) Projector (10%) (b) Charts (15%)
2. You have gone to field trips, Educational tours.	Yes (26%) No (74%)	Yes (16%) No (84%)	Yes (32) No (78)

As the Table–4.22 shows audiovisual aids were moderately used in the classrooms. Students belonging to Arts and Humanities said that maps (24%), projector (8%) and charts were used. Science students said that slides (13%), projector (6%) and charts (8%) were used. Commerce students said that projector (10%) and charts (15%) were used.

Similarly, most of the students did not go to field trips and educational tours and the percentage of which stood at 80. However, it was Commerce students who went to field trips (32%) while it was marginal with Science, Arts and Humanities students.

Table–4.23

STUDENTS' VIEWS

Regarding Problems of Autonomous Colleges (No = 130)

Statement	*Students in*		
	Arts & Humanities	*Science*	*Commerce*
1	*2*	*3*	*4*
1. State the problems of autonomous colleges.	(a) Syllabus has been completed in a hasty way (19%). (b) Part- time jobs and other activities cannot be taken up as we are so preoccupied with studies (6%). (c) There are no problems. I don't know much (8%). (d) We find it difficult to be tuned to system (3%). (e) The degree certificates issued by autonomous colleges do not carry much weight (15%).	(a) Syllabus has been completed in a hasty way (18%). (b) Part- time jobs and other activities cannot be taken up as we are so preoccupied with studies (5%). (c) There are no problems (7%). (d) Lecturers are biased (2%). (e) The degree certificates issued by autonomous colleges do not carry much weight (14%).	(a) Syllabus has been completed in a hasty way (18%). (b) Part- time jobs and other activities cannot be taken up as we are so preoccupied with studies (3%). (c) There are no problems (4%). (d) Lecturers are biased (2%). (e) The degree certificates issued by autonomous colleges do not carry much weight (8%).

(Contd...)

1	2	3	4
	(f) Students studying in affiliated colleges talk lightly of the marks obtained (16%). (g) Teachers punish and ill-treat us (2%) (h) The periods allotted to the lecturers are not sufficient to complete the syllabus (38%). (i) Sometimes lecturers do not give attendance in spite of our coming to college (7%). (j) Classes are held even in April and May (18%). (k) Students do not bother about the syllabus when the semester is over (16%). (l) Subjects have not been learnt thoroughly (16%). (m) Internal Assessment and mid semester examinations become problematic (38%).	(f) Students studying in affiliated colleges talk lightly of the marks obtained (13%). (g) Teachers punish and ill-treat us (4%) (h) The periods allotted to the lecturers are not sufficient to complete the syllabus (28%). (i) Classes are held even in April and May (18%). (j) Students do not have time to take coaching outside (12%). (k) Students do not take note of the syllabus after the completion of the semester (36%). (l) Subjects have not been learnt thoroughly (14%). (m) Internal Assessment and mid semester examinations become problematic (34%). (n) Classes are held in Summer (17%).	(f) Students studying in affiliated colleges talk lightly of the marks obtained (6%). (g) Teachers punish and ill-treat us (2%) (h) The periods allotted to the lecturers are not sufficient to complete the syllabus (26%). (i) Sometimes lecturers do not give attendance in spite of our coming to college (7%). (j) Classes are held even in April and May (15%). (k) Students do not have time to take coaching outside (10%). (l) Students do not bother about the syllabus when the semester is over (25%). (m) Subjects have not been learnt thoroughly (15%). (n) Internal assessment and mid semester examinations become problematic (40%).

As per the Table–4.23, Arts and Humanities, Science and Commerce students made the following observations when they were asked to give their views regarding the problems confronted by autonomous colleges. They opined that syllabi had been completed in a hasty way. Part- time jobs and other activities could not be taken up, as we are so preoccupied with studies. A few others said that they did not know much. Some students replied that they found it difficult to be tuned to system.

The following are the students' other replies: the degree certificates issued by autonomous colleges did not carry much weight. Students studying in affiliated colleges talked lightly of the marks obtained. Teachers punished and ill-treated us. The periods allotted to the lecturers were not sufficient to complete the syllabus. Sometimes lecturers did not give attendance in spite of their coming to college. Classes were held even in April and May. Students did not bother about the syllabus when the semester was over. Subjects had not been learnt thoroughly. Internal assessment and mid semester examinations became problematic. Only a few science students remarked that the lecturers were prejudiced. Barring one or two problems, all the students irrespective of their streams of study, spotted the same problems.

As the Table–4.24 shows, (*See on pages 84-86*) students made the following observations when they were asked to give suggestions for the success of autonomous colleges.

Arts and Humanities students opined that there should be an emphasis on self-preparatory notes which could be possible when a few hours per week were set apart for library (76%). Seminars, which were organized, should be useful to the students (20%). Internal evaluation should be unbiased. Syllabi should be properly planned bearing in mind the future interests of the students and the demands of employment market (72%). Marks should not be allotted to attendance (13%). Answer scripts should be given back to the students (11%). Lecturers should be friendly with the students (12%). Sports and cultural activities should be given their due share (9%). Measures should be taken to bring about some awareness in computers (14%). Autonomous colleges should have some more powers (6%). The certificates issued by the college should be given value on par with the certificates secured by non-autonomous colleges (13%). Syllabus should be limited so that lecturers can complete them in the hours allotted to them (15%). A few holidays should be given prior to examinations (10%). Fundamentals of a subject should be imparted in the first year. In the second and the third years there should be proper extension of basic knowledge (18%).

Science students observed that there should be an emphasis on self -preparatory notes and this could be possible when a few hours per week were reserved for library (68%). There should be some special syllabi so that we could fare well in the world of competitive examinations (22%). Marks allotted to internal examinations should be decreased (30%). Shift system may be introduced. Internal evaluation should be unbiased. Syllabi should be properly planned bearing in mind the future interest of the students and the demands of employment market (71%). Lecturers should be friendly with the students (7%). Sports and cultural activities should be given their due share (8%). Autonomous colleges should have some more powers (6%). Syllabus should be limited so that lecturers can complete them in the hours allotted to them (17%). Fundamentals of a subject should be important in the first year. In the second and the third years there should be proper extension of basic knowledge (18%).

Commerce students opined that there should be an emphasis on self- preparatory notes which can be possible when a few hours per week are set apart for library (65%). Internal evaluation should be unbiased (25%). Syllabi should be properly planned keeping in mind the future interest of the students and the demands of employment market (73%). There should be proper management and effective execution of programmes (16%). There should be good staff (15%). Students should possess duty, devotion, and dedication (13%). There should be congenial educational atmosphere (3%). Answer scripts should be given back to the students (4%). There should be sufficient time to prepare well end semester examinations (6%). Lecturers should be friendly with the students (2%). Sports and cultural programmes should be given their due share (13%). Autonomous colleges should have some more powers (7%). Syllabus should be limited so that lecturers could complete them in the hours allotted to them (12%). Fundamentals of a subject should be imparted in the first year. In the second and the third years there should be proper extension of basic knowledge (6%). It is striking to note that students while making observations for successful implementation of autonomy, touched upon all the focal issues regarding college autonomy.

Table–4.24

STUDENTS' VIEWS

Regarding Suggestions for the Success of Autonomous Colleges (No = 130)

	Students in		
Statement	*Arts & Humanities*	*Science*	*Commerce*
1	*2*	*3*	*4*
1. Suggestions for improving the functioning of autonomous colleges.	(a) There should be an emphasis on self-preparatory notes which can be possible when a few hours per week are set apart for library (76%). (b) Seminars, which are organized, should be useful to the students (20%). (c) Internal evaluation should be unbiased (22%)	(a) There should be an emphasis on self-preparatory notes which can be possible when a few hours per week are set apart for library (68%). (b) There should be some special syllabi so that we can fare well in the world of competitive examinations (22%). (c) Marks allotted to internal examinations should be decreased from 50% to 30% (30%).	(a) There should be an emphasis on self-preparatory notes which can be possible when a few hours per week are set apart for library (65%). (b) Internal evaluation should be unbiased (25%). (c) Syllabi should be properly planned bearing in mind the future interest of the students and the demands of employment market (73%).

(Contd...)

1	2	3	4
	(d) Syllabi should be properly planned bearing in mind the future interest of the students and the demands of employment market (72%). (e) Marks should not be allotted to attendance (13%). (f) Answer scripts should be given back to the students (11%). (g) Lecturers should be friendly with the students (12%). (h) Sports and cultural activities should be given their due share (9 %). (i) Measures should be taken to bring about some awareness in computers (14%).	(d) Shift system may be introduced. Internal evaluation should be unbiased. (e) Syllabi should be properly planned bearing in mind the future interest of the students and the demands of employment market (71%). (f) Lecturers should be friendly with the students (7%). (g) Sports and cultural activities should be given their due share (8%). (h) Autonomous colleges should have some more powers (6%). (i) Syllabus should be limited so that lecturers can complete them in the hours allotted to them (17%).	(d) There should be proper management and effective execution of programmes (16%). (e) There should be good staff (15%). (f) Students should possess duty, devotion, and dedication (13%). (g) There should be congenial educational atmosphere (3%). (h) Answer scripts should be given back to the students (4%). (i) There should be sufficient time to prepare well for end semester examinations (6%).

(Contd...)

1	2	3	4
	(j) Autonomous colleges should have some more powers (6%). (k) The certificates issued by the college should be given value on par with the certificates secured by non-autonomous colleges (13%). (l) Syllabus should be limited so that lecturers can complete them in the hours allotted to them (15%). (m) A few holidays should be given prior to examinations (10%). (n) Fundamentals of a subject should be imparted in the first year. In the second and the third years there should be proper extension of basic knowledge (6%).	(j) Fundamentals of a subject should be imparted in the first year. In the second and third years there should be proper extension of basic knowledge (18%).	(j) Lecturers should be friendly with the students (2%). (k) Sports and cultural programmes should be given their due share (13%). (l) Autonomous colleges should have some more powers (7%). (m) Syllabus should be limited so that lectures can complete them in the hours allotted to them (12%). (n) Fundamentals of a subject should be imparted in the first year. In the second and the third years there should be proper extension of basic knowledge (12%).

Table–4.25

PRINCIPALS', LECTURERS' & STUDENTS' VIEWS

Regarding Reliability of Evaluation (No = 196)

Statement	*Principal*	*Lecturers*	*Students*
1	2	3	4
1. The reliability of internal assessment is often questioned by the students.	Yes No (100%)	Yes (9%) No (91%)	Yes (88%) No (12%)
2. You consider that the internal assessment is unbiased.	Yes (100%) No	—	Yes (80%) No (20%)
3. There is provision to improve the marks obtained in internal assessment	Yes No (100%)	Yes No (100%)	—
4. There are some other problems with the evaluation.	—	(a) Teachers are not adequately trained in test construction and so the testing is by and large unsatisfactory. (30%)	(a) The average marks of the two internals have been given. But it is good if they take the better of the two into consideration (18%).

(Contd...)

1	2	3	4
		(b) Evaluation (marking) has been done perfunctorily since each teacher is burdened with a large number of answer scripts. (29%) (c) Need to increase more objectivity in evaluation. (34%) (d) Some times question papers are known to the students before the exams. (5%) (e) Students should be evaluated only academically without taking attendance into consideration (11%) (f) Objective type questions are to be increased to make evaluation more objective. (23%)	(b) Valuation of the scripts should be fair and perfect. (19%) (c) Only one mid exam should be conducted. Seminars and assignments should be given adequate weightage. (26%) (d) It is difficult for N.C.C and N.S.S students to get permission particularly when the exams are going on. (2%) (e) Percentage of marks in the final exams comes down as the internal marks are added to it. (13%) (f) Syllabi have been completed in a slipshod manner. (15%) (g) Students are overburdened with examinations (19%). (h) Students are goaded to do endless variety of work. (14%). (i) Students have little time to look after anything besides examinations. (23%) (j) We have little time to play (30%).

Table–4.25 shows that the autonomous colleges affiliated to A.N.U follow semester system. The principals and lecturers felt that the students did not often question the reliability of internal assessment. However, students' perception regarding internal assessment was somewhat different. Some felt that internal assessment was unbiased.

Nevertheless, there was no provision to improve the marks obtained in internal assessment. When asked whether there were any problems with internal evaluation, the principals replied in the negative.

But the lecturers and students identified some problems regarding internal evaluation.

The problems specified by the lecturers were that they were not adequately trained when it comes to test construction, evaluation. Some lecturers felt that the scripts had been valued perfunctorily. There was need to increase objectivity in evaluation, the need to introduce objective type of questions in order to making evaluation more objective.

The students opined that it was good to take into consideration the better marks secured by the students in one of the two internals; that the valuation should be fair and perfect; that one internal is enough; that the continuous internal examinations precipitated speedy coverage of the syllabi; that students were goaded to do endless variety of work; that they have no time either to look after anything besides examinations or to play. It can be seen that the problems spotted by the lecturers and the students were not alike but then they delved deep into different aspects of evaluation.

Table–4.26

PRINCIPALS', LECTURERS'& STUDENTS' VIEWS

Regarding Educational Technology (No = 196)

Statement	*Principals*	*Lecturers*	*Students*
1	2	3	4
1. You are making use of audio-visual aids.	Yes (100%) No	Yes (68%) No (32%)	—
2. Name the audio-visual aids used in the classroom.	—	—	Projector (8%) Maps (8%) Charts (10%) Slides (4%)
3. There is some scope for learner-centered instruction in the classroom.	Yes (100%) No	Yes (76%) No (24%)	Yes (22%) No (78%)
4. Kindly state the other innovative practices introduced in learning process.	1. Group discussion (100%) 2. Project work (100%) 3. Student-seminars (100%) 4. Assignments (100%)	1. Group discussion (24%) 2. Project work. (14%) 3. Seminars. (100%) 4. Assignments to students. (25%) 5. Self-study in some subjects (56%) 6. Field trips (18%) 7. Continuous internal assessment (100 %) 8. Workshops (30 %) 9. Management games (7%) 10. Production of instructional material by the members of (English) Department. (6%) 11. Problem solving sessions (50%)	—

As can be seen from the above Table–4.26, all the principals replied that the lecturers were making use of audio-visual aids. It was said that there was scope for learner-centred instruction in the classroom. The other innovative practices introduced in the classroom were group discussion, project work, student seminars and assignments.

It can be seen from the table above that Arts and Commerce lecturers were using audio-visual aids moderately. Science lecturers were availing them to the maximum extent possible (96%). According to many lecturers in Arts and Science disciplines, there was scope for learner–centred instruction in the classroom. However, almost all the lecturers felt that there was scope for learner-centered instruction. There were many innovative teaching practices introduced by lecturers belonging to Arts, Humanities, Commerce and Science. They were, to mention a few, seminars, self-study, group discussions, workshops, production of instructional material, project work, management games, etc.

Students replied that audio-visual aids were used marginally. They were confined to maps, slides, projector and charts. Many students said that they were not taken out for field-trips and other educational tours.

The Table–4.27 (*See on next page*) juxtaposes the views of principals, lecturers and students of autonomous colleges on the problems of autonomous colleges.

The principals concurred that there had been delay in releasing the normal assistance. They added that the university should allow them to do what they wanted. Some lecturers said that university and the state government were indifferent to the problems confronted by them.

Table–4.27

PRINCIPALS', LECTURERS'& STUDENTS' VIEWS

Regarding Problems of Autonomous Colleges (No = 196)

Statement	*Principals*	*Lecturers*	*Students*
1	*2*	*3*	*4*
1. Kindly state the problems of autonomous colleges.	(a) Delay in releasing normal assistance by UGC (100%) (b) Designing courses relevant to society is very difficult (100%). (c) University should allow us to do what we want (100%).	(a) Indifference of the university and the state government (60%) (b) Absence of networking of autonomous colleges (26%) (c) Some universities would not like to take into consideration the marks obtained in internal assessment (70%).	(a) Syllabus has been completed in a hasty way (18%). (b) Part-time jobs and other activities cannot be taken up, as we are so pre occupied with studies (5%). (c) There are no problems. We don't know much. (6%) (d) We find it difficult to be tuned to the system (1%).

(Contd…)

1	2	3	4
		(d) Too much workload (64%) (e) Inadequacy of academic staff (16%). (f) Academic staff being not properly trained in syllabus design, teaching methodology and testing (44%). (g) If lecturers become inactive and uncommitted to the academic work autonomy will collapse (36%). (h) If the lecturers do not upgrade their knowledge system fails (28%). (i) Ad-hoc teaching staff problems need to be addressed (52%). (j) Co-curricular activities have not been given their due share (16%). (k) Autonomy to P.G. courses should be granted (44%)	(e) The degree certificates issued do not carry much weight. Students studying in affiliated colleges talk lightly of the marks obtained. (12%). (f) Lecturers are biased (2%). (g) Teachers punish and ill-treat us (13%). (h) Sometimes lecturers do not give attendance in spite of our coming to college (5%). (i) The periods allotted are not enough to complete the syllabus (31%). (j) Classes are held even in April and May (17%). (k) Students do not have time to take coaching outside. (21%).

(Contd…)

1	2	3	4
		(l) Lack of research activity (32%) (m) The system curtails student's freedom (28%) (n) Students become more positive participants (32%)	(l) Students do not bother about the syllabus when the semester is over (26%). (m) Subjects have not been learnt in-depth. (15%). (n) Internal Assessment and mid-semester examinations are problematic. (37%)

Lecturers expressed the following views pertaining to the problems being faced in autonomous colleges. They are: indifference of the university and the state government; absence of networking of autonomous colleges; some universities would not like to take into consideration the marks obtained in internal assessment; too much workload; inadequacy of academic staff; academic staff being not properly trained in syllabus design, teaching methodology and testing; if lecturers became inactive and uncommitted to the academic work autonomy would collapse; if the lecturers did not upgrade their knowledge system fails; ad-hoc teaching staff problems need to be addressed; co-curricular activities had not been given their due share; autonomy to P.G. courses should be granted; lack of research activity ; the system curtailed students freedom; students became more passive participants.

Students expressed different views with regard to the problems being confronted in autonomous colleges. They are: syllabus had been completed in a hasty way; part-time jobs and other activities could not be taken up as we were so preoccupied with studies; there were no problems; we don't know much; we found it difficult to be tuned to the system; the degree certificates issued did not carry much weight; students studying in affiliated colleges talked lightly of the marks obtained; lecturers are biased; teachers punish and ill-treat us; sometimes lecturers did not give attendance in spite of our coming to college; the periods allotted to the lecturers were not suffice to complete the syllabus; classes were held even in April and May; students did not have time to take coaching outside; students did not bother about the syllabus when the semester was over; subjects had not been learnt in-depth; internal assessment and mid–semester examinations became problematic.

Table–4.28

PRINCIPALS', LECTURERS'& STUDENTS' VIEWS

Regarding Suggestions for the Success of Autonomous Colleges (No = 196)

Statement	*Principals*	*Lecturers*	*Students*
1	2	3	4
1. Kindly give some suggestions for the success of college autonomy.	(a) Foolproof examination system (100%) (b) Committed and dedicated staff and rapport among them (100%). (c) The UGC and the state government should respect the spirit of autonomy (100%).	(a) Complete autonomy should be granted in academic matters i.e. starting of new courses, restructuring of existing courses based on need and opportunities available (96%) (b) Semester system should be implemented (72%) (c) Ratio of internals should not exceed (56%). (d) Co-operation between government, autonomous colleges and the UGC.	(a) There should be an emphasis on self-preparatory notes which can be possible when a few hours per week are set apart for library (69%). (b) Seminars, which are organized, should be useful to the students (27%). (c) Internal evaluation should be unbiased (27%). (d) Syllabi should be properly planned bearing in mind the future interest of the students and the demands of employment market (72%). (e) Marks should not be allotted to attendance (4%).

(Contd...)

1	2	3	4
		(e) Absolute freedom has to be given to departments to structure and restructure syllabi (20%). (f) Proper planning (48%). (g) The workload of teachers may be reduced enabling them to introduce innovations like projects, surveys and field work as part of the curriculum and supervise them effectively (80%). (h) Teachers of Autonomous colleges should be properly trained in syllabus design, teaching methodology and testing (72%). (i) Refresher courses for teachers in ACs. (28%).	(f) Answer scripts should be given back to the students (5%). (g) Lecturers should be friendly with the students (6%). (h) Sports and cultural activities should be given their due share (6 %). (i) Measures should be taken to bring about some awareness in computers (5%).

(Contd...)

1	2	3	4
		(j) The UGC may organize curriculum development renewal programmes for autonomous colleges with suitable resource persons (36%). (k) ASC should come forward to orient teachers in new areas (28%). (l) Service conditions of the lectures appointed on the ad-hoc basis should be improved (18%). (m) Examinations must be conducted fool-proof (72%).	(j) Autonomous colleges should have some more powers. (4%). (k) The certificates issued by the college should be given value on par with the certificates secured by non-autonomous colleges (4%). (l) Syllabus should be limited so that lecturers can complete them in the hours allotted to them (13%). (m) A few holidays should be given prior to examinations (3%).

(Contd...)

1	2	3	4
		(n) Co-operation between the staff and management and understanding between students and staff (68%). (o) Encouragement to teachers who introduce innovative teaching practices (32%). (p) Industry-college interaction and as per the need, syllabi should be up-dated (20%). (q) Support for meaningful research (11%). (r) Job-oriented courses should be introduced (25%)	(n) Fundamentals of a subject should be imparted in the first year. In the second and the third years there should be proper extension of basic knowledge (6%).

The Table–4.28 gives us the suggestions put forward by principals, lecturers and students for the success of college autonomy.

The principals were of the view that the foolproof examination system committed and dedicated staff and rapport among them, honouring the spirit of autonomy by the UGC and the state government.

The lecturers on the other hand felt that complete autonomy should be granted in academic matters i.e. starting of new courses, restructuring of existing courses based on need and opportunities available. Semester system should be implemented. The percentage of marks given to internals should not exceed. There should be co-operation between government, autonomous colleges and the UGC. Absolute freedom had to be given to departments to structure and restructure syllabi. There should be proper planning. Most of the lecturers held that the workload of teachers may be reduced enabling them to introduce innovative measures like projects, surveys and field work as part of the curriculum and supervise them effectively. Teachers of autonomous colleges should be properly trained in syllabus design, teaching methodology and testing. There should be refresher courses for teachers in autonomous colleges. The UGC may organize curriculum development renewal programmes for autonomous colleges with suitable resource persons. Academic staff colleges should come forward to orient teachers in new areas. Service conditions of the lecturers appointed on the ad-hoc basis should be improved. Examinations must be conducted foolproof. Co-operation between the staff and management and understanding between students and staff was of great importance. Encouragement should be given to teachers who introduced innovative teaching practices. There should be industry-college interaction and according to the needs, syllabi should be up-dated. There should be support for meaningful research. Job-oriented courses should be introduced.

The perspectives of students are diametrically different from those of principals and lecturers as far as the measures to be taken up for the success of college autonomy are concerned. They opined that there should be an emphasis on self- preparatory notes which can be possible only when a few hours per a week are set apart for library. Seminars, which are organized, should be useful to the students. Internal evaluation should be unbiased.

It is worthwhile to see their observations pertaining to syllabi. They viewed that it should be properly planned bearing in mind the future interests of the students and the demands of employment market. Marks should not be allotted to attendance. Answer scripts should be given back to the students. Lecturers should be friendly with the students. Sports and cultural activities should be given their due share. Measures should be taken to bring about some awareness in computers. Autonomous colleges should have some more powers. The certificates issued by the college should be valued on par with the certificates secured by non-autonomous colleges. Syllabus should be limited so that lecturers can complete them in the hours allotted to them. A few holidays should be given prior to examinations. Fundamentals of a subject should be imparted in the first year. In the second and the third years there should be proper extension of basic knowledge.

The analysis brings out the fact that there is a need to introduce some reforms, and bring in a few drastic and radical changes in the existing college autonomy, which will be discussed in the next chapter based on the conclusions inferred.

5

SUMMARY, CONCLUSIONS AND DISCUSSIONS

It has been universally acknowledged that Indian higher education is extremely rigid, incapable of accommodating the fluctuating demands of a vibrant society. There are some anachronistic practices which have become a drag affecting the quality of higher education. Certain practices like the affiliating system which was borrowed from Britain vanished from the country of its origin. The colonial masters authored the scheme as it suited to their interests. Even after independence, the government continues to conform to the same policies as a result of which universities tend to show less concern for academic programmes and concentrate more on administrative functions. Many suggestions have been offered to effect positive changes in the collegiate education. Of these, the conferment of autonomy to colleges has been a significant step to improve the quality of higher education. According to the University Grants Commission, college autonomy has the potential to pave way for academic excellence. An autonomous scheme as documented in the UGC Guidelines (1998) will give the institution "the freedom to devise its curriculum, evolve more effective methods of teaching and learning, and revise rules of admission to suit its aims, conduct its own programmes of assessment and examination and to undertake other specific programmes in order to achieve academic excellence."

Autonomous colleges are meant to send out batches of bright students who have the required skills to get absorbed in the job-market. These colleges are supposed to give a fillip to the enterprising teachers to pursue academic goals and take them off from the stronghold of conservatism, and the resultant inertia of the affiliating system. Congenial academic atmosphere can be created and benchmark practices for generating new ideas and activities can be developed easily in an autonomous institution. The scheme of college autonomy can be a success when the college is able to translate the goals.

The main objectives of an autonomous college are many and varied. In its pursuit of knowledge, it helps the development of its community in its neighbourhood and the society at large. It is supposed to ensure the employability of the students. This involves the introduction of employment-oriented and vocational-based educational courses and programmes. Thus it is incumbent upon it to make education functional, productive, meaningful and relevant. The main functions of an autonomous institution are as follows: development of courses and curricula to satisfy the needs and aspirations of local people; maintenance of academic standards; adopting modern and challenging methods of instructions. Accordingly, the college shall have freedom to determine its own courses of study and syllabi, prescribe rules of admission subject to the reservation policy and to evolve methods of evaluation to conduct examinations.

It is interesting to note that there are three separate agencies involved in the matter of conferment of autonomy on the colleges which have to function under the rules and regulations of these three agencies. They are the parent university which gave autonomy; the state government which concurred with the UGC's proposal for granting autonomy, and the UGC which gave the concurrence as well as the necessary instruction to the parent university to grant autonomy. When a college has switched over to autonomy it has to bind to the above three. In a sense, its autonomy is confined and qualified owing to the interference of the above three.

Autonomous scheme was devised to empower an institution to optimize all its resources and scale the rungs of excellence. True to the spirit of the scheme, they have blazed a trail of academic achievements in the realm of higher education. However, they are functioning under a number of constraints. To name a few, at the time of granting autonomy, the UGC promised special financial assistance to the colleges to develop proper infrastructure etc., but the assistance is not time-bound. The UGC delays the sanctioning of these grants in time. Apart from this, the autonomous colleges cannot bring in the necessary reforms in courses, curricula, etc., unless permission from the parent university and the state government concerned are accorded. Besides these, autonomous colleges have confronted a plethora of other problems. To aggravate the problems further, the inadequacies on the part of the individuals involved are glaring. To put it in a nutshell, practice of autonomy is at variance with the scheme of autonomy. Unless these problems are addressed and causes unravelled, college autonomy is not going to be successful.

The present study is intended to address the dilemmas and problems being confronted by autonomous colleges at various levels within the institution and outside. However, owing to the constraint of time and meagre resources, the researcher has to confine the study to some specified problems. These had been identified after consulting the academicians of repute and the Revised UGC Guidelines. Keeping the constraints in mind, a few variables like principals, lecturers and students belonging to various disciplines and colleges have been taken into consideration. A few other variables, the Managements of the two colleges, the Dean of College Development Council and the officials of the UGC who are supposed to oversee the functioning of college autonomy, were omitted from the study as they did not return the questionnaires.

Two principals, sixty four lecturers and one hundred and thirty students were included in the sample of the study. An open-ended questionnaire was framed for the present study with different statements. Frequencies were used to infer conclusions from the raw data obtained from the principals, the lecturers and the students. Importance is given to solicit pertinent information rather than to stringent research procedures.

CONCLUSIONS AND DISCUSSION

The following are the conclusions drawn from the analysis of data. The conclusions follow the discussion which is aimed at suggesting some remedies to mitigate the major problems of autonomous colleges. These suggestions are inferred from the observations made by the subjects—the principals, the lecturers and the students and various committees and commissions on higher education.

1. **The principals, lecturers and most of the students saw the need of starting job-oriented courses.**

The principals, lecturers and students have opted for job-oriented and more practical combination of courses which will entail the success both of the students and of the institutions. The ground reality in higher education is that students show some tilt towards those courses which ensures employability and handsome salary packages and many of the traditional courses fail to meet the yardstick. There has been a steep decline in terms of admission and students are not willing to join the streams of sciences, commerce and arts. This has been the trend for long and this precipitates the closure of many sections in the institutions of south India. In consonance with the changing scenario of globalization of education, therefore, the colleges may have to reorient and reshape their policies and programmes to make the instruction more relevant and career-oriented with focus on "quality and excellence" as the UGC has pointed out in its Guidelines on college autonomy. It is envisaged that professionally qualified graduates with a sound knowledge of their core subjects and expertise in a skill concerned will have better chances in the sectors of service, industry and other avenues in self-employment. The UGC likes to encourage in introducing career and market-oriented, skill-enhancing courses that will have bright chances of employment and empowerment.

Since autonomous colleges have freedom to design the courses, they are supposed to offer a wide range of career-oriented courses in various related areas. For this purpose, a centre for Career-Oriented Entrepreneurship may be established because it will be a focal point for developing curriculum, resource materials for various programmes and organizing workshops for training the faculty. It also helps in giving support, facilities in training and placement of students. Thus it will assume the responsibility for the implementation and development of employment-oriented courses. Further, students may be facilitated to achieve a minimum level of competencies for moving into the employment market or in self-employment. To realize this objective, some vocational course spanning about one to three years may be integrated with the degree.

Under-graduate students fail to carve out a place for themselves in the world of employment because there is a divorce between general education and vocational education. In this context, it is worthwhile to refer to the Kothari Commission's report which says that there should not be greater distinction between vocational and general education. The element of vocational education should have some place in general education. National Knowledge Commission (2006) struck the same chord when it says: "The creation of knowledge cannot be directionless. To derive maximum benefits from our intellectual assets, we must apply knowledge in fields like agriculture, industry, health, education, etc., where productivity can be enhanced. Knowledge application is both a goal in itself and a facilitator of progress in these important sectors". This goal can be realized when job-oriented courses are structured into the academic programmes of the autonomous institution. In other words, a judicious combination of vocational and general courses is the panacea to the problem of unemployment which figures prominently when it comes to students pursuing general courses. Such a measure will provide some corrective to the over-academic nature of formal education.

It is a general complaint that students from rural and semi-urban areas are lacking in the soft-skills even though they are quite good at their academics. In order to enhance employability of its wards, the institutions are also supposed to organize bridge courses that impart communication skills and training in personality development. Besides some other important ingredients, these courses include skills for career planning, leadership, assertiveness, interpersonal communications, group communication, comprehension, effective writing, creative writing, decision-making and creative thinking.

2. Post-graduation departments need autonomy

There is some resentment from some quarters that the university has not given autonomy to P.G. departments. The academic programmes run by the autonomous colleges may be viewed in totality. If an autonomous college can successfully implement autonomy at U.G. level, it can safely be surmised that the college can competently implement the autonomous scheme at P.G. level as well. Hence, the university and State Council for Higher Education may not dither in granting autonomy to P.G. courses too. To qualify for the autonomy at P.G. level, the colleges may scrupulously follow the UGC rules regarding the qualifications of the faculty, their appointments and pay scales.

3. The principals, the lecturers and the students felt that foolproof system of examination is vital for the success of autonomy

The foolproof system of examination is very crucial. Since autonomous colleges have to conduct examinations on their own, they should have to be on the alert lest conducting examinations should become a farce and the credibility of marks would be at stake. Therefore, they should devise ways and means to hold examinations in a foolproof manner. New technologies which would enhance objectivity with little human interference may be used to make the system more reliable and valid.

4. Importance should be given to academic innovations and educational technology

Even the best of the curricula can be made a dead letter if the teaching is not activity-based. In fact, autonomous college scheme has been viewed as the principal mechanism to ensure enhancement of quality by introducing academic innovations besides weeding out weak and bad colleges which mechanically follow the obsolete traditional courses and practices. It would make a mockery of autonomous system if an autonomous college tinkers its academic programmes and practices merely imitating the programmes of an affiliating university or some other autonomous colleges. This would give a fatal blow to college autonomy. Therefore, innovative practices should be encouraged. The emphasis on teaching should be shifted from verbalism and memorization to learning through purposeful, concrete and realistic situation. For this purpose, the principles of Project Method should be assimilated in learning situations. A more learner-oriented or enquiry-oriented teaching method should be introduced in the instructional system which enables the learner to engage himself in creative and divergent thinking, problem solving, self-learning and exploring new avenues of communication and productive work.

The importance of audio-visual aids in an autonomous college assumes a great role. The teacher, besides knowing the recent development in his subject, is supposed to keep in touch with the new methods. Even while designing syllabi, the people concerned should bear in mind to suggest the various aids to be used. They accelerate the rate of learning outcome as they have a great appeal. They enable the teacher to teach less and learner to learn more. Hence, education technology may be given its due share to optimize learning process. Focusing on e-learning strategies for diverse needs and learning styles is the need of the hour. The changing pattern of education demands practical-oriented learning. It must be accelerated and broadened by the use of many and varied devices and materials.

The advent of information technology, electronically delivered educational services, real-time television and computer links may prove to make interactive learning possible. The new emerging online Web 2.0 technologies such as weblogs, wikis, moodles, folkonomies, m-learning, podcasting, vodcasting, virtual worlds, etc., have become potential educational tools today. Scientific experiments, some of which are expensive, can be conducted making use of computer-aided technology as these colleges have good computer laboratories. The institutions may make use of simulations, as they are excellent learning tools. The users can negotiate environmental constraints, and witness the effects of changes in variables. The interactive multimedia packages on the internet can simulate complex work experiences through games as critical tools to evaluate the kind of skills that are so often difficult to measure in tests. They underscore the importance of E-Teacher.

5. There should be a consortium of autonomous colleges

It has been found that the colleges in question did not forge any alliance with any other autonomous colleges and this may lead to their virtual academic isolation. In an age of technology and democracy, it is neither desirable nor possible to remain insulated. The institutions should learn to co-operate and collaborate without sacrificing quality. Co-operation and collaboration should lead to mutual enrichment. Hence, the autonomous institutions have to consult some other institution or institutions when a problem crops up. But then, it may be proper to give the exchange some legitimacy that will expedite mutual exchange of information in a smooth and transparent manner. This can be possible when some mechanism is worked out. Hence, there should be networking of autonomous colleges. In fact, the UGC itself has suggested that there should be a consortium of autonomous colleges which will facilitate the exchange of novel ideas, staff, etc. When colleges are passing through initial phases of autonomy, such help would be immensely beneficial.

Autonomous colleges flourish better when they share their experiences and expertise by forming into a consortium. At least colleges under the jurisdiction of a university may organize themselves under one umbrella. Herein lays the crucial role of the university because it can mobilize at least the colleges under its jurisdiction to form a network of autonomous colleges, which have remained so far as islands far flung.

Here, it is pertinent to refer to the Ramamurthy Committee's recommendation that the state governments and the universities should hold regular meetings with the principals of autonomous colleges for co-ordination and resolving issues. Further, such co-ordination facilitates transfer of students from one institution to the other. It is pertinent to observe here that the higher educational institutions are very aggressively active in opening their off-shore campuses and are ready to twin with other institutions in other countries. Very serious competition from foreign institutions looms large on the horizon. One of the ways to tide over the problem is to forge some alliance with the strong institutions and evolve some workable norms to work with them, if possible. Loyola College, Chennai, for instance, has tackled the challenge by forging tie-ups with universities and renowned organizations to offer educational programmes and to enhance students' employability. In 2006 and 2007 alone it forged MoUs with institutions like London South Bank University, London, Lillie Catholic University, France, (2006) Southerland Global Services Private Limited (2007), etc. This calls for qualities like promptitude, intellectual agility and courage and a propensity to take upon challenges.

6. Some lecturers put forward the suggestion that there should be separate orientation courses for lecturers working in autonomous colleges

Keeping in view of the general academic programmes of the lecturers working in autonomous colleges, Academic Staff Colleges should come forward to orientate lecturers in the new areas because change of syllabi has lately become a very dynamic process. In a sense, monitoring, controlling and improving quality in an educational institution has always been difficult for autonomous colleges. Hence, it is incumbent on the part of academic staff colleges to devise courses for the teachers emphasizing on revised syllabi so that they can handle the classes more effectively. Sometimes a course may be completely restructured. In such a case, failure to orientate the staff may cost dearly. These measures need expertise and special focus. Hence, the autonomous colleges may ponder over entrusting the new responsibility to Internal Quality Assurance Cell without waiting for help.

7. The service conditions of the unaided lecturers have to be ameliorated

It goes without saying the tone and character of life in a country is conditioned largely by the tone and quality of its colleges, which depend primarily upon the quality of teachers. Besides laying stress on their personal traits and educational qualifications, emphasis should also be on their service conditions.

A lecturer who is in dire straits may not contribute much to the educational process. Therefore, it is highly imperative that their services should be regularized and salaries be adequately hiked.

Owing to the lackadaisical policies of the state government the number of the unaided lecturers is on the increase. In many of the colleges they have outnumbered aided lecturers. Since the job of an unaided lecturer continues to be temporary, they may leave the college pursuing some lucrative jobs. As a result, college autonomy may get affected because new lecturers take time to grasp the new system and so it is hard to get into the groove. Even these lecturers may go out in search of greener pastures. Hence, there is a need to keep them in the fold.

It is obligatory on the part of the managements to implement the UGC pay scale if lecturers are qualified as per the norms. It is tantamount to academic apartheid if some enjoy the UGC pay scales and the rest fail to eke out their livelihood. Such an atmosphere is a fertile ground for breeding jealousies and could set off other negative thought processes. The same work and the same pay should be the dictum here. If it is beyond their means the managements may have to see the feasibility of introducing the Triple Benefit Scheme i.e., pension-cum-provident fund-cum-insurance as recommended by Indian Education Commission. The UGC and state government may enhance allocation of funds remarkably to those colleges which have implemented such a scheme. No doubt, it is an onerous task entailing financial commitment. The task becomes greater as these aided institutions are service-oriented and may not function like corporate colleges squeezing exorbitant fees from the students. Hence, it is incumbent on the part of the government to vigorously support the aided institutions which are accredited at the A or B levels. Nevertheless, the institutions may initiate measures and strategies to ensure their financial autonomy which has become indispensable in the face of liberalized economic world where the invasion of foreign universities is going to be an awful reality. Institutions which have substantial financial resources and intellectual dynamism to change for the better can only prosper. Devising self-financing courses to raise revenue and putting its infrastructure to optimum use are some of the ways to ensure financial autonomy.

8. Students should not be over-disciplined

One of the grave charges against internal evaluation, mid-term examinations and other tests is that they are wielded as weapons to discipline students. In order to avoid victimization, the institutions may adopt various strategies like question banks prepared by the external examiners. Even photocopies of the answer papers on some payment may be given to students because transparency increases the reliability of evaluation system. In addition, the Grievances Appeals Committee is geared up to solve the students' grievances with minimal procedural bottlenecks. It is not possible to teach by coercion; the goodwill of the people involved in the system is always essential. It can be ensured by effective teamwork. There should be teamwork between the principal and the staff; lecturers and lecturers; lecturers and students; students and students; and among principal, lecturers and students. Secondly, a suitable programme of co-curricular activities gives the students a sense of social co-operation, makes them self-directing, develops an insight into the boons of order and discipline, heightens the respect for the people in authority thereby providing fine training in leadership.

True, discipline is the most vital aspect of the college administration; it is the control of behaviour, the subjugation of emotions and action under the direction of a leader in fulfillment of certain aims. Since there has been a considerable reaction against authoritarian discipline, it may be kept in mind that people should be led to discipline themselves. Students should be counselled the value of intrinsic discipline by suitable professionals.

It can be ensured that good traditions, well-planned team-work, unified discipline policy, a suitable programme of co-curricular activities, well-conducted assemblies, personal contact, good college premises, well-furnished library, specialized rooms and a better standard student-supporting services make students profitably busy and keep them away from indiscipline. So discipline emphasized should be of positive and creative type.

The appointment and creative functioning of various joint committees headed by the principal, as The Education Commission has observed, can generate a spirit of comradeship between teachers and students. It may be kept in mind that autonomy should also percolate to students. Discipline can be maintained if the centre of authority is shifted from the teacher to the entire class. It has been held that democratic type of discipline has a very high educative value because every individual is aware of self-imposed control which is the highest form of discipline. Only academicians of high repute endowed with patience, perseverance and resourcefulness can make it possible.

9. Need-based and job-oriented courses will not lose their value when there is linkage between institution and industry

It has been held that linkage between industry and institution is of great importance. As long as collegiate education imparts theoretical perspectives and the concept of higher education is reduced only to passing of examinations, the question may not raise. When it comes to the need-based and job-oriented courses, nevertheless, the autonomous colleges may not devise them keeping in mind the local demand. If such is the case, the colleges may go for the courses which have demand in their next immediate environment. Further, there is scope for wider links between the colleges and the world of work in terms of joint research activities, technology transfer, consultancy, sharing of equipment, solving technical problems and development programmes. Continuous relations with the industries can be maintained by inviting their representatives to participate creatively on boards of Academic Council, Executive Council and the like. The colleges may be in touch with some bodies like The Science and Technology Entrepreneurs Programme (STEP). In fact, STEP is a good example to show how higher educational institutions could organize the industry-linked programmes.

The aim of a college is to make its students not only knowledgeable but also employable. When the industry is going to introduce modern technology, or make some changes, the college can either add or omit the lessons. Thus providing "wholesome fare" can ensure their employability. When courses are upgraded, restructured and reviewed periodically and when there is no divide between an industry and an institution the relevance of the job-oriented courses will never be lost.

10. Some lectures felt that there should be training for lecturers working in autonomous colleges in syllabus design, curriculum development and testing

The faculties of autonomous colleges need to spruce up their knowledge continuously because syllabus design is a challenging task calling for pragmatic approach. Ultimately, it is the design of syllabus which bears testimony of the nature and worth of a college. Syllabus should have an international touch about it. In fact, knowledge is getting international with a vengeance. The ripe wisdom of the ancient Greeks was accessed during the renaissance period effected phenomenal changes in the western world bringing material prosperity. The world is dwindling into a tiny place, a global village and hence, there is an urgent need to internationalize the curricula in conformity with the international standards. It is apt to say that international higher education has become a giant industry. Institutions of the developed countries would like to start their academic programmes across the world. The college cannot afford to falter owing to a faulty or out-dated syllabus design. Much discussion should takes place. After keeping abreast of the recent trends and emerging issues, designing relevant syllabus can be possible.

Some lecturers consider the necessity of training programmes encompassing the various needs of autonomous colleges. The areas which need training are syllabus design, teaching methodology, etc. They suggested that among other things, the above should be taught in Refresher Courses specially designed for lecturers working in autonomous colleges. The training will not go waste, as it is helpful in designing and restructuring the syllabus and other important things. In addition to them, the UGC may direct State Higher Educational Council and Parent University to organize Curriculum Development Programmes for autonomous colleges with suitable resource persons. The colleges may also conduct some seminars or refresher courses at regular intervals bearing in mind the demands of new academic programmes.

If syllabus is designed nonchalantly and testing is conducted in a slip-shod manner it would be disastrous to the students. The image of the college ultimately rests on the academic courses being run and programmes being chalked out. So much thought should go into them before finalizing them. It is only with the wiliing experts of the university departments and others distinguished themselves in their spheres concerned, syllabus can effectively be designed. The restructured syllabus has to be restructured periodically.

11. The principals felt that there was delay of normal assistance by the UGC to autonomous colleges

Every year the UGC gives normal financial assistance to autonomous colleges to meet their additional and special needs. It has been held that there is an inordinate delay in the release of funds. The delay seems to be unavoidable as the UGC releases the assistance based on the previous year's expenditure incurred by an autonomous college. Since the implementation of some programmes entails huge funds, the commission may see the feasibility of releasing about 75 per cent of the normal assistance of the previous year.

12. There are no differences between a minority autonomous college and an open-ended autonomous college and among the lecturers and students belonging to various disciplines

The problems being confronted have been spotted the same, and hence no divergence of views among the subjects of the sample.

13. Principals, lecturers and students of the autonomous college held that an autonomous college was better than an affiliated college

Everyone with one accord agrees that the merits of college autonomy far outweigh those of affiliating system. The reasons for the preference are obvious. Autonomous colleges can creatively experiment and explore the validity of various issues bearing on students' future. Purposeful syllabus designing, continuous internal assessment, changing the academic programmes and bringing in reforms in the whole process of teaching-learning situation in consonance with the changing times are some of the merits of college autonomy.

However, the debatable question is how far the stakeholders in autonomous system strive to realize the ideals of college autonomy. Since they are shouldering all the responsibilities which had long been borne by the university in an apathetic way, they should be active and enterprising in academic pursuits exploiting the optimum utilization of resources available. There must be rapport among the members of staff. If they lack good attributes of head and heart, college autonomy for name's sake does not serve any purpose.

14. The workload of the lecturers may be reduced so that they can engage themselves in other academic activities and introduce innovations like projects, surveys and fieldwork and supervise them effectively

It is noteworthy to see that despite the relative heavy workload the lecturers would not like to back off from college autonomy on that account and this was evidenced from their preference for autonomous system. However, most of the lecturers in the autonomous colleges are grousing about the workload. It is obvious that compared to the lecturers working in an affiliated college, lecturers of an autonomous college have to look after a host of activities besides classroom teaching. These include conducting seminars, correcting the assignments given to the students, conducting the mid semester examinations, continuous evaluation, evaluating the scripts, taking part in various decision making and welfare committees. All these are considered cumbersome and an extra burden. Besides, the summer vacation or other festival vacations have to be drastically narrowed down. Among other reasons, perhaps, the lecturers are not happy because they cannot have leisure for academic pursuits.

The Education Commission has suggested that conditions of work in educational institutions should be improved so as to enable the teachers to function at the highest level of efficiency. Further, the commission has suggested that non-teaching work, such as co-curricular activities, tutorials, etc., should also be taken into account. The quality and competence of the teachers is appraised more valuable in maintaining high quality education and its contribution to national development. Nothing is more important than providing them with the best possible preparations and creating satisfactory conditions of work. Further, the lecturers in the affiliated colleges shrink back from the autonomous system feeling that they will have to cow down under the burden of work pattern.

Various decisions of the government to woo market forces and World Bank make the institutions shudder at the thought of appointing staff because it entails some financial burden. The burden becomes inevitable, for instance, in the context of the GO. 35 issued by the A.P. government. In a disguised fashion, it puts a virtual ban on filling vacancies. The GO has given a lethal blow to the aided institutions and it is very unlikely that the government will annul it. As Andhra Pradesh has been lauded as a government to initiate reforms right from the former Chief Minister, N. Chandrababu Naidu, there is every possibility of other states taking its cue. One cannot impose the principles of market economy on every sector inextricably linked to the well-being of people at large. In intermediate education the so-called corporate culture has already set in. It does not let any other institution-government or aided-survive. Paradoxically, it has started devouring even small and relatively gigantic institutions. There is utter chaos reigning supreme in intermediate education as the state government ruthlessly follows the policy of cutting down expenditure. It is very likely to extend the same policies in the domain of higher education. This kind of bungling of delicate issues has become rampant across the country, more so in Andhra Pradesh. The government's callous treatment becomes more stringent as days pass by as a result of which the managements, the muted spectators, find it difficult to address the problem. These institutions are the result of decades of sustained hard work, intellectual courage and vision of great educationalists and philanthropists. It is ironical to note that while western developed countries are keen on protecting many that come under GATT agreement, our governments do not show such maturity in crucial issues of decision-making. Speaking in the ACTA Diamond Jubilee celebrations at Bhimavaram, Andhra Pradesh, in July 2007 K.C. Reddy, Chairman of Andhra Pradesh State Council of Higher Education tried to dispel the teachers' doubts when he said that the Council has recommended that aided system be continued as the aided institutions cater to the poorer sections (70% of which include S.C, S.T. and B.C) of society. But there are no visible signs of such measures. If the government follows the same policies, the institutions along with the common man bog down into the mire of problems. Some of the institutions may run on the lines of market economy. But the layman cannot. The government should stop speechifying on the efficacy of the privatization of basic services lest all will incur the wrath of the common man. Live and let live should be the philosophy of any economy.

It is, therefore, reasonable to feel that the government should give freedom for these colleges to fill the vacancies of academic, non-academic and auxiliary nature. It may evolve separate norms of workload for lecturers working in autonomous colleges after taking into account the working pattern of various faculties.

15. Autonomous colleges sought more academic, administrative and financial autonomy

No one can dispute the fact that college autonomy thrives on freedom and self-government. An autonomous institution can charter its way successfully if it is bestowed upon freedom. The UGC and the parent university should, therefore, give autonomous colleges some rope so that they can create congenial atmosphere and academic culture of superior type. There may be, however, some bureaucratic control to ward off certain elements and other narrow-minded people who are clamouring for more autonomy. They may subvert autonomy for their ulterior purposes. Autonomy of this sort will prove to be detrimental to the secular fabric of the country. Nor can autonomy mean the liberty to create financial requirements without making any serious attempts at raising internal resources. Hence, there should be some bureaucratic control without impinging upon the intrinsic freedom of the institution and without letting the control degenerate into extortionate delay in releasing funds and the consequent autocracy.

Freedom cannot be interpreted as the liberty to follow its ill-conceived plans without any checks and balances. No system can thrive on lack of discipline, which masquerades as autonomy.

Efforts should, therefore, be made to find out a golden mean between autonomy and bureaucratic control to ensure the benchmark practices of college autonomy. In this connection, it is pertinent to recollect the recommendations of Education Commission. It says that educated planning should be the right blend of centralization and decentralization. There should be national plans, state plans, and institutional plans and they should fit into each other.

The UGC and the parent university are supposed to see that autonomy should enable a college to enjoy genuine creative freedom to design appropriate academic programmes, teaching strategies and evaluation techniques that are learner-oriented. In the garb of autonomy, the government should not disown its responsibility to withdraw financial support. The rumour has been doing rounds that the Andhra Pradesh government has tacitly come to an understanding with the World Bank to the effect of which it would stop financing the aided institutions in gradual phases. The GO 35 of Andhra Pradesh issued on 27-03-06 corroborates the fact that privatization of higher education is an impending reality. The institutions cannot afford to live in some utopia expecting some benign treatment. The autonomous institutions in particular should swing into action and step up measures that would ensure financial autonomy.

The government is supposed to give a second thought to its plan to withdraw financial support. Such a plan would result in the exorbitant hike in the fee structure. The common man cannot afford the fee. These colleges cater to the needs of economically weaker sections of society. Here it is important to observe that these institutions which are creditably accredited at the "A" level have been performing exceedingly well. The colleges may find it difficult to pool resources to pay salaries to the staff. As a result, the college autonomy may tumble down. It is important to note that autonomy is a joint pursuit involving students, teachers and the management with the active support of the government, parent University and the UGC.

16. Students felt that a few hours per week should be set apart for library hours

The Kothari Commission said that the goal of undergraduate education of the first degree is to bring students "to the frontiers of knowledge and threshold of the world of research". It is disheartening to see that the first-degree colleges do not come up to these standards. As the document Challenge of Education (1985) points out, a large majority of the "colleges are engaged in mere ritual of teaching." There is little scope for self-study. The students just rely on notes being dictated by their lecturers and guidebooks. No wonder the students lag in communication skills, and have only limited knowledge, information and worldview. Therefore, it is highly imperative to see students visit library or on-line library and to have access to the world of information. Students thus can prepare the notes or material on their own. Here the teachers' role is that of a facilitator making comments, correcting their notes, asking the students to exchange their notes, and monitoring them while they are doing the work. This paradigmatic shift from teacher-centred learning to student-centered learning turns them into autonomous learners.

17. The autonomous colleges did not implement cafeteria model of Choice-based Credit System (CBCS). The principals and lecturers did not find fault with it

The two terms "Choice" and "Credit" emphasize the interests and aspirations of the learner on the one hand and the demands of the academic system on the other, which the learner has to meet. When a comparison is made between the present system and credit-based curriculum, one can quickly realize where the present system has gone wrong. Here workload is mostly determined on the basis of lecture hours for each course of study. Each lecture is meant to "cover" the syllabus and coaches the learner for an examination. The lecture cannot "challenge" the learner to do the creative work using a student's aptitude and talent. It does not provide for student-work within the schedule. Even written work in the form of assignments, seminar reports, record work, etc., is haphazardly done because the government does not consider it necessary to calculate the workload. When it comes to western countries, the time allotted to lectures is less than that allotted for student work. Furthermore, it is obligatory on the part of autonomous colleges to conform to the UGC Guidelines regarding the implementation of credit system. Nevertheless, while going for credit system, it should be borne in mind that a mere conversion of marks into credits and withholding of student course options do not make a credit system.

18. Some lecturers and many students felt that the marks/ certificates obtained in the autonomous colleges did not carry much weight outside

An autonomous college worth its salt cannot afford to ignore this sort of criticism. If such is the problem, it should devise ways and means to make its certificates worthy. After ascertaining the veracity of such remarks, measures should be taken to overhaul the internal assessment in particular and the whole system in general with a committee of experts. While working out the modalities of courses, the members of the Board of Studies are supposed to bear in mind the local needs and global standards. They should make higher education globally relevant. The yardstick of comparability will be of immense value here. UK's Dearing Committee Report holds that the education offered in any part of the globe ought to be so sound and quality oriented that it is relevant in any other part of the globe. This observation has more relevance in the globalized world.

Hence, the institutions cannot be complacent by showing a high student pass rate. The changing context demands institutions of a new order—dynamic, vibrant, quality-conscious. Then only they can assure the quality of their output. An excellent syllabus may be framed—good students, good library facilities, and proper management of the examination system—but all are in vain if motivated teachers are not around. In an autonomous college much depends on the teachers who are in charge of imparting education to the students. The teachers can easily slip into self-complacence when they lack academic dynamism. They should try to be on par with university teachers in terms of qualifications, achievements and expertise.

An autonomous college as an organization is a sea where people with different backgrounds, skill-sets, academic qualifications and personalities come together. Success cannot be ensured when the individuals work in isolation. This will result in academic inertia. With remarkable perspicacity, therefore, the different individuals should be engaged in the learning process which is a collective endeavour. A successful organization is the one which recognizes the diversity and utilizes it to the optimum level.

19. Co-curricular activities should be given more importance

Co-curricular activities, it has been held, have not been given their due share in the colleges where generally utmost importance is given to "covering syllabus." The activities are of great magnitude as they cover all facets of development-pattern and ensure harmonious development. Hence, co-curricular activities should be conceived as part and parcel of the curricula. There is no gainsaying the fact that the pursuit of desirable, different interests gives zest for life, broadens one's horizons, supplements and enriches classroom experiences and provides an excellent background for the profitable use of leisure. Not infrequently, such pursuit affects vocational choices besides promoting good physical and mental health. So a variety of wholesome co-curricular activities may be organized and promoted on the college campus.

20. Lecturers belonging to the autonomous colleges felt that students with the aid of lecturers should undertake research projects

Research should have its due share in the academic programmes of the college. When its wards pursue higher education strenuously, new ideas germinate which find fertile soil in research. Though research activity may be beyond the capacity of undergraduate students, it is neither impractical nor impossible provided proper training and encouragement are given. In fact, undergraduate students should have a foretaste of research as the Kothari Commission has remarked. At least those students who are keen and have an aptitude for research may be identified so that they can be encouraged to take up some project work. It will be beneficial to both the lecturers and the students as it hones their skills and helps them identify their area of interest at later stage.

Above all, a college can carve a niche for itself when it really contributes something to knowledge. Such contribution may be made when its students undertake research with all vigour and verve. It is apt to add here that Loyola College, Chennai, though it is a teaching college, has consistently enhanced its research profile by receiving awards and funding to initiate researches in different departments. Their researches contribute enormously to an effective teaching. It is not out of place to state that that they are 17 ongoing projects , the money amounting to Rs. 1,92,59,755/-. This corroborates the need to cultivate an aptitude for research not only by students but by lecturers as well.

College autonomy will be a roaring success when the institutions march ahead with sincerity of purpose to serve the economically backward sections of society. An autonomous institution can make its mark when it offers various scholarships and concessions to bright students to the tune of 50 per cent to 75 per cent depending on their financial viability of its resources. Top rankers may be accommodated under the scholarship scheme and more such schemes can be initiated with the support of new endowments, parent teacher associations, and alumni associations. Such supporting services, and the special schemes like "earn while you learn" are the need of the hour. In the face of inexorable forces of liberalization and globalization, these autonomous colleges of repute at least, to some extent, may shoulder some social responsibility.

To conclude, knowledge has assumed the form of intellectual property and countries imparting high quality education can on their own emerge triumphant and reap the fruits of the new GATT agreement. Indeed, the agreement paved way for the globalization of economy and this likely to lead globalization of higher education. Foreign institutions can thrive when the autonomous institutions lack the vigour and vision. Hence, these institutions should equip themselves to stem in the tide of invasion of foreign universities. It becomes imperative for the autonomous institutions to reflect on the aspects discussed and see for themselves how they can attempt at them by evolving suitable strategies and strive to realize the prescribed targets and avowed objectives of excellence.

SUGGESTIONS FOR FURTHER RESEARCH

Research is a continuous process. Some other relevant areas strike the researcher during the work. In light of the results of the present study, the following research studies may be taken up:

1. The sample selected for the present study is not wide enough in its scope. It is, therefore, recommended to take up a detailed study taking a wider sample;

2. An investigation may be undertaken to study the roles of other variables like chairpersons of various committees in autonomous colleges;

3. Studies may be taken up to identify the role of the U.G.C, State Council of Higher Education, and University in the functioning of college autonomy;

4. A comparative study may also be taken between the problems of autonomous colleges of one university with those of others;

5. A study confined to the problems of a particular area of college autonomy may yield better results;

6. An exclusive study on the functioning of important committees in the main may be undertaken since they have great bearing on the tenor of the college;

7. In order to find out the actual progress and strides made in terms of academic innovations, a separate study may be done on the college autonomy being practised and the affiliating system that was practised;

8. A study may be done in a comprehensive manner, the autonomous practices of our country and those of others in another country or countries.

BIBLIOGRAPHY

Altbach, Philip, G.A. Critique of Higher Education. *Hindu:* Hyderabad, 12 April, 2005.

Amrik Singh, "No More Babysitting, Please", *Tribune,* 1 Jan. 2005.

Basu, A.N. (1957), *Education in Modern India.* Calcutta: Orient Book Co.

Boyles, Earnest E. (1966), *Pragmatism in Education.* New York: Harper Collins.

Bhaskara Rao, Digumarthi, ed. (1996), *National Policy on Education,* 2 Vols. New Delhi: Anmol Publications Pvt. Ltd.

Bhaskara Rao, Digumarthi, ed (1997), *Education for the 21st Century.* New Delhi: Discovery Publishing House.

Best, John W (1992), *Research in Education,* 8ed. New Delhi: Prentice-Hall of India Pvt. Ltd.

Brubacher, John S. (1961), *Modern Philosophies of Education.* Englewood Cliffs, N.J.: Prentice Hill Inc.

Cobban, A.B. (1975), *The Midieval Universities: Their Development and Organization.* London: Methuen.

Deshmukh K.G. (1998), "Universities and Higher Education in the 21st Century", *University News,* Vol. 36 No. 28.

Geoffrey (1996), "Audit, Assessment and Academic Autonomy", *Higher Education Quarterly.*

Government of India. *Report of the Education Commission (1964-66)*, New Delhi: Government Printing Press.

http://www.sssindia.org. *View Point Six* (A Joint Publication of Centre for Civil Society and Kerala Higher Education Forum).

http://www.ugc.ac.in/financial *Revised Guidelines on the Scheme of Autonomous Colleges* (1998) UGC, New Delhi.

John, V.V (1976), *Freedom to learn: The Challenges of Autonomous Colleges*, Delhi: Vikas Publishing House.

Kamala Bhatia (1992), *Philosophical and Sociological Foundations of Education*. Tenth Impression. Delhi: Doaba House.

Kilpatrick, William H. ((1963), *Philosophy of Education*. New York: Macmillan.

Kundai Swami,V.C. "Reconstruction of Higher Education". *Hindu* 18 May, 2005.

Kundu, C.L. and Gupta L.C.(1993). *Autonomous Colleges: Concept and Implementation*. New Delhi: Sterling Publishers Pvt. Ltd.

Lavakare P.J., Gulati S.K. (1995), "Exporting Higher Education: Opportunities and Challenges", *Journal of Higher Education*, Vol. 18.

Mir Ayoob Alikhan, *Rural Students Take Over OU*. Deccan Chronicle. Hyderabad, 23, Jan. 2006.

Neelamegham, S. (2000), *Professional Competency in Higher Education*. Delhi. University of Delhi.

Olivia, M. "Quality Enhancement Initiatives in Higher Education". *University News*, XXXIX, September, 2001.

Ottoway, A.K.C. (1969), *Education and Society*. London: Routledge and Kegan-Paul.

Pala Prasada Rao V. *"The Learning Outcome of Weblogs – Some Issues."* A Paper Presented at International Conference on New and Emerging Technologies in ELT at Loyola College, Chennai, 3-5 August, 2007.

_____. *"Placement Cell in Our College – Some Experiences."* A Paper Presented at the National Seminar on Healthy Practices, Their Impact and Student Participation" at V.S.R. & N.V.R. College, Tenali, 25-26 February, 2007.

Power K. B. (1995), "Higher Education in India: Historical Perspective, Present, Status and Outlook for the Future", *University News*, Vol. 33 No. 6.

Ramachandra Rao R. *The Crisis in Higher Education*. Hindu. Vijayawada, 11, August, 2006.

Raza Moonis (1991), *Higher Education in India*. New Delhi: Association of Indian Universities.

Russell, Bertrand (1928), *Education and the Good Life*. New York: Boni and Leverright.

Saiyidain, K. G. (1969), *The Humanist Tradition in Educational Thought*. Madison: Denbar.

Schultze, Theodore W. (1967), *The Economic Value of Education*. New York: Harper and Row.

Seabury Paul (1981), *Bureuucrats and Brain Power: Government Regulation of University*", American Journal of Education, Vol. 89, No. 2.

Singh, Avadesh Kumar. "Contextualising Higher Education in India". *University News*, XXXXL, August, 2007.

Sharma and Mangal S.K. (1998), *Fundamentals of Educational Research*. Meerut: International Publishing House.

Sudha Rao,K. "*College Autonomy Facts and Impacts*": Orientation Programme Reading Material. Delhi: Jamia Millia Islamia, 2001.

Terry, Mark (1971), *Teaching for Survival*. New York: Ballantine Books.

Xavier Alphonse, "The Agony and Ecstasy of College Autonomy". Chennai: *New Frontiers of Education* XXXVIII No.1, January-March, 2003.

REFERENCES

Bhaskara Rao, Digumarti (1994), ***Scientific Aptitude***, New Delhi: Ashish Publishing House. ISBN 81-7024-658-X.

Bhaskara Rao, Digumarti (1995), ***Animal Kingdom***, New Delhi: Discovery Publishing House. ISBN 81-7141-274-2.

Bhaskara Rao, Digumarti (1995), ***Batracology,*** New Delhi: Discovery Publishing House. ISBN 81-7141-279-3.

Bhaskara Rao, Digumarti (1997), ***Scientific Attitude,*** New Delhi: Discovery Publishing House. ISBN 81-7141-381-1.

Bhaskara Rao, Digumarti (1996), ***Scientific Attitude vis-à-vis Scientific Aptitude,*** New Delhi: Discovery Publishing House. ISBN 81-7141-308-0.

Bhaskara Rao, Digumarti (2004), ***Scientific Attitude, Scientific Aptitude and Achievement,*** New Delhi: Discovery Publishing House. ISBN 81-7141-781-7.

Bhaskara Rao, Digumarti (2004), ***Educational Administration,*** New Delhi: Discovery Publishing House. ISBN 81-7141-842-2.

Bhaskara Rao, Digumarti (2004), ***Issues in School Education.*** New Delhi: Discovery Publishing House. ISBN 81-8356-025-3.

Bhaskara Rao, Digumarti, Editor (1996), ***Encyclopaedia of Education For All,*** 5 Volumes. New Delhi: APH Publishing Corporation. ISBN 81-7024-759-4 (set).

Vol. I ***Education For All*: The World Conference,** ISBN 81-7024-760-8.

Vol. II ***Education For All*: The EPA-9 Summit,** ISBN 81-7024-761-6.

Vol. III ***Education For All*: Quality Education For All,** ISBN 81-7024-762-6.

Vol. IV ***Education For All*: Planning and Monitoring,** ISBN 81-7024-763-4.

Vol. V ***Education For All*: The Indian Scenario,** ISBN 81-7024-764-0.

Bhaskara Rao, Digumarti, Editor (1996), ***National Policy on Education,*** 2 Volumes, New Delhi: Anmol Publications Pvt. Ltd. ISBN 81-7488-323-1.

Bhaskara Rao, Digumarti, Editor (1996), ***Global Perceptions on Peace Education,*** 3 Volumes, New Delhi: Discovery Publishing House. ISBN 81-7141-319-6.

Bhaskara Rao, Digumarti, Editor (1997), ***Education for the 21st Century,*** New Delhi: Discovery Publishing House. ISBN 81-7141-389-7.

Bhaskara Rao, Digumarti, Editor (1997), ***Reflections on Scientific Attitude,*** New Delhi: Discovery Publishing House. ISBN 81-7141-319-6.

Bhaskara Rao, Digumarti, Editor (1997), ***Success Story of a Primary Education Project,*** New Delhi: APH Publishing Corporation. ISBN 81-7024-850-7.

Bhaskara Rao, Digumarti, Editor (1997), ***World Food Summit,*** New Delhi: Discovery Publishing House. ISBN 81-7141-386-2.

Bhaskara Rao, Digumarti, Editor (1997), ***Care the Child,*** 2 Volumes, New Delhi: Discovery Publishing House. ISBN 81-7141-394-3.

Bhaskara Rao, Digumarti, Editor (1998), ***Earth Summit,*** 2 Volumes, New Delhi: Discovery Publishing House. ISBN 81-7141-435-4.

Bhaskara Rao, Digumarti, Editor (1998), ***Adolescence Education,*** New Delhi: Discovery Publishing House. ISBN 81-7141-432-X.

Bhaskara Rao, Digumarti, Editor (1998), ***Community and School Nutrition Education,*** New Delhi: Discovery Publishing House. ISBN 81-7141-435-4.

Bhaskara Rao, Digumarti, Editor (1998), ***District Primary Education Programme,*** New Delhi: Discovery Publishing House. ISBN 81-7141-396-X.

Bhaskara Rao, Digumarti, Editor (1998), ***National Policy on Education: Towards an Enlightened and Humane Society,*** New Delhi: Discovery Publishing House. ISBN 81-7141-426-5.

Bhaskara Rao, Digumarti, Editor (1998), ***Reforming School Education,*** New Delhi: Discovery Publishing House. ISBN 81-7141-403-6.

Bhaskara Rao, Digumarti, Editor (1998), ***Teacher Education in India,*** New Delhi: Discovery Publishing House. ISBN 81-7141-406-0.

Bhaskara Rao, Digumarti, Editor (1998), ***World Summit for Social Development,*** New Delhi: Discovery Publishing House. ISBN 81-7141-420-6.

Bhaskara Rao, Digumarti, Editor (1999), ***International Encyclopaedia of AIDS,*** 11 Volumes. New Delhi: Discovery Publishing House. ISBN 81-7141-522-6 (set).

Vol. 1 ***Introduction to HIV/AIDS,*** ISBN 81-7141-523-7.

Vol. 2 ***HIV/AIDS – Issues and Challenges,*** 2 Parts, ISBN 81-7141-524-5.

Vol. 3 ***HIV/AIDS – Socio-Economic Realities,*** ISBN 81-7141-524-3.

Vol. 4 ***HIV/AIDS – Law, Ethics and Human Rights,*** 2 Parts, ISBN 81-7141-526-1.

Vol. 5 ***AIDS and NGOs,*** ISBN 81-7141-527-X.

Vol. 6 ***AIDS and Home Care,*** ISBN 81-7141-528-8.

Vol. 7 ***STD Case Management,*** ISBN 81-7141-529-6.

Vol. 8 ***HIV/AIDS Prevention and Care – Teaching Modules for Nurses and Midwives,*** ISBN 81-7141-530-X.

Vol. 9 ***HIV Prevention Education for Educational Institutions,*** ISBN 81-7141-531-8.

Vol. 10 ***Instructional Modules for AIDS Education,*** ISBN 81-7141-532-6.

Vol. 11 ***School Health Education to Prevent AIDS and STD – A Package for Curriculum Planners,*** ISBN 81-7141-533-4.

Bhaskara Rao, Digumarti, Editor (2000), ***International Encyclopaedia of Human Rights,*** 7 Volumes in 13 Parts, New Delhi: Discovery Publishing House. ISBN 81-7141-567-9 (set).

Vol. 1 ***International Instruments of Human Rights,*** 2 Parts, ISBN 81-7141-569-4.

Vol. 2 ***Regional Instruments of Human Rights,*** ISBN 81-7141-604-7.

Vol. 3 ***Human Rights and the United Nations,*** 2 Parts, ISBN 81-7141-605-5.

Vol. 4 *Fact Files of Human Rights,* 3 Parts, ISBN 81-7141-606-3.

Vol. 5 *Study Stories of Human Rights,* 3 Parts. ISBN 81-7141-607-3.

Vol. 6 *International Meetings on Human Rights,* 2 Parts. ISBN 81-714-608-X.

Vol. 7 *Professional Training in Human Rights,* ISBN 81-7141-609-8.

Bhaskara Rao, Digumarti, Editor (2000), ***International Encyclopaedia of Science and Technology Education,*** 11 Volumes, New Delhi: Discovery Publishing House. ISBN 81-7141-548-2 (set).

Vol. 1 *Science and Technology Education,* ISBN 81-7141-568-7.

Vol. 2 *Science Education in Developing Countries,* ISBN 81-7141-569-9.

Vol. 3 *Organizational Structure of Science,* ISBN 81-7141-570-9.

Vol. 4 *Science Education in Asia and the Pacific,* ISBN 81-7141-571-7.

Vol. 5 *Science and Technology Education For All,* ISBN 81-7141-572-5.

Vol. 6 *Values, Ethics, Talent and Girls in Science and Technology Education,* ISBN 81-7141-573-3.

Vol. 7 *Popularization of Science and Technology Education,* ISBN 81-7141-574-1.

Vol. 8 *Science, Power and Society,* ISBN 81-7141-575-X.

Vol. 9 *Information Technology,* ISBN 81-7141-576-8.

Vol. 10 *Teacher Training in Science and Technology Education,* ISBN 81-7142-577-6.

Vol. 11 *Teacher Training in Science and Technology: A Curriculum Framework,* ISBN 81-7141-578-4.

Bhaskara Rao, Digumarti, Editor (2000), ***Education For All: Achieving the Goal,*** 3 Volumes. New Delhi: APH Publishing Corporation. ISBN 81-7648-152-1 (set).

Vol. I ***The Global Consensus.*** ISBN 81-7648-155-6.

Vol. II ***Mid-Decade Review Reports of Regional Seminars,*** ISBN 81-7648- 154-8.

Vol. III ***Issues and Trends,*** ISBN 81-7648-155-6.

Bhaskara Rao, Digumarti, Editor (2001), ***Nuclear Materials: Issues and Concerns,*** 2 Volumes, New Delhi: Discovery Publishing House. ISBN 81-7141-611-X.

Bhaskara Rao, Digumarti, Editor (2001), ***Distance Education in Different Countries,*** New Delhi: APH Publishing Corporation. ISBN 81-7648-229-3.

Bhaskara Rao, Digumarti, Editor (2001), ***Decentralised Management of Education: Management of Education in Panchayati Raj and Municipal Bodies,*** New Delhi: Discovery Publishing House. ISBN 81-7141-617-9.

Bhaskara Rao, Digumarti, Editor (2001), ***Electrochemistry for Environmental Protection,*** New Delhi: Discovery Publishing House. ISBN 81-7141-619-5.

Bhaskara Rao, Digumarti, Editor (2001), ***Global Educational Studies,*** New Delhi: Discovery Publishing House. ISBN 81-7141-616-0.

Bhaskara Rao, Digumarti, Editor (2001), ***Global Synthesis of Educational Assessment,*** New Delhi: Discovery Publishing House. ISBN 81-7141-613-6.

Bhaskara Rao, Digumarti, Editor (2001), ***Jomtein Decade of Education,*** New Delhi: Discovery Publishing House. ISBN 81-7141-618-7.

Bhaskara Rao, Digumarti, Editor (2001), ***World Conference on Education for All,*** New Delhi: APH Publishing Corporation. ISBN 81-7648-274-9.

Bhaskara Rao, Digumarti, Editor (2001), ***World Conference on Higher Education,*** New Delhi: Discovery Publishing House. ISBN 81-7141-610-1.

Bhaskara Rao, Digumarti, Editor (2001), ***World Conference on Science,*** New Delhi: Discovery Publishing House. ISBN 81-7141-612-8.

Bhaskara Rao, Digumarti, Editor (2003), ***Inspiring Experiences in Teacher Education,*** New Delhi: Discovery Publishing House. ISBN 81-7141-656-X.

Bhaskara Rao, Digumarti, Editor (2003), ***International Studies in Education,*** 3 Volumes. New Delhi: Discovery Publishing House. ISBN 81-7141-647-0.

Bhaskara Rao, Digumarti, Editor (2003), ***Military Conversion: Impact on Science and Technology,*** New Delhi: Discovery Publishing House. ISBN 81-7141-578-4.

Bhaskara Rao, Digumarti, Editor (2003), ***United Nations Millennium Summit,*** New Delhi: Discovery Publishing House. ISBN 81-7141-632-2.

Bhaskara Rao, Digumarti, Editor (2003), ***World Assembly on Aging,*** New Delhi: Discovery Publishing House. ISBN 81-7141-637-3.

Bhaskara Rao, Digumarti, Editor (2003), ***World Conference on Human Rights,*** New Delhi: Discovery Publishing House. ISBN 81-7141-661-6.

Bhaskara Rao, Digumarti, Editor (2003), ***World Education Forum,*** New Delhi: Discovery Publishing House. ISBN 81-7141-639-X.

Bhaskara Rao, Digumarti, Editor (2003), ***Education, Employment and Human Resource Development,*** New Delhi: Discovery Publishing House. ISBN 81-7141- 681-0.

Bhaskara Rao, Digumarti, Editor (2003), ***Successful Schooling,*** New Delhi: Discovery Publishing House. ISBN 81-7141-677-2.

Bhaskara Rao, Digumarti, Editor (2003), ***European Education and Teachers,*** New Delhi: Discovery Publishing House. ISBN 81-7141-702-7.

Bhaskara Rao, Digumarti, Editor (2003), ***Teachers in a Changing World,*** New Delhi: Discovery Publishing House. ISBN 81-7141-694-2.

Bhaskara Rao, Digumarti, Editor (2004), ***International Guidelines on Open and Distance Teacher Education***, New Delhi: Discovery Publishing House. ISBN 81-7141-777-9.

Bhaskara Rao, Digumarti, Editor (2004), ***Adult Learning in the 21st Century***, New Delhi: Discovery Publishing House. ISBN 81-7141-797-3.

Bhaskara Rao, Digumarti, Editor (2004), ***Educational Practices: Research and Recommendations***, New Delhi: Discovery Publishing House. ISBN 81-7141-835-X.

Bhaskara Rao, Digumarti, Editor (2004), ***General Secondary Education In the 21st Century***, New Delhi: Discovery Publishing House.

Bhaskara Rao, Digumarti, Editor (2004), ***International Encyclopaedia of Learning to Live Together***, 4 Volumes, New Delhi: Discovery Publishing House. ISBN 81-7141-848-1.

Vol. 1 ***International Conference on Learning to Live Together.***

Vol. 2 ***Globalization and Living Together.***

Vol. 3 ***Curriculum for Learning to Live Together.***

Vol. 4 ***Science Education for the Contemporary Society.***

Bhaskara Rao, Digumarti, Editor (2004), ***Reforming Secondary Education***, New Delhi: Discovery Publishing House. ISBN 81-7141-843-0.

Bhaskara Rao, Digumarti, Editor (2004), ***Human Rights Education***, New Delhi: Discovery Publishing House. ISBN 81-7141-882-1.

Bhaskara Rao, Digumarti, Editor (2004), ***United Nations Decade for Human Rights Education***, New Delhi: Discovery Publishing House. ISBN 81-7141-887-2.

Bhaskara Rao, Digumarti, Editor (2004), ***Technical and Vocational Education and Training in the 21st Century***, New Delhi: Discovery Publishing House. ISBN 81-7141-984-4.

Bhaskara Rao, Digumarti, Editor (2005), ***Encyclopaedia of Education For All***, 5 Volumes. New Delhi: Discovery Publishing House.

Bhaskara Rao, Digumarti and B.S.V. Dutt, Editors (2003). **Education: Programmes and Policies.** New Delhi: APH Publishing Corporation. ISBN 81-7648-470-9.

Bhaskara Rao, Digumarti, C.A.P. Swamy and B.S.V. Dutt (1997), ***Self-Evaluation in Student Teaching,*** New Delhi: Discovery Publishing House. ISBN 81-7141-374-9.

Bhaskara Rao, Digumarti and D. Naresh Kumar (2004), ***School Teacher Effectiveness,*** New Delhi: Discovery Publishing House. ISBN 81-7141-782-5.

Bhaskara Rao, Digumarti and D. Sridhar (2002), ***Job Satisfaction of School Teachers,*** New Delhi: Discovery Publishing House. ISBN 81-7141-652-7.

Bhaskara Rao, Digumarti, C. Sridevi and K. Vijaya (1995), ***Achievement in Social Studies,*** New Delhi: Discovery Publishing House. ISBN 81-7141-281-5.

Bhaskara Rao, Digumarti and Digumarti Pushpa Latha (1994), ***Achievement in Biology,*** New Delhi: Discovery Publishing House. ISBN 81-7141-264-5.

Bhaskara Rao, Digumarti and Digumarti Pushpa Latha (1995), ***Achievement in English,*** New Delhi: Discovery Publishing House. ISBN 81-7141-283-1.

Bhaskara Rao, Digumarti and Digumarti Pushpa Latha (1994), ***Achievement in Science,*** New Delhi: Discovery Publishing House. ISBN 81-7141-280-70.

Bhaskara Rao, Digumarti and Digumarti Pushpa Latha (1995), ***Achievement in Mathematics,*** New Delhi: Discovery Publishing House. ISBN 81-7141-278-5.

Bhaskara Rao, Digumarti and Digumarti Pushpa Latha (2004), ***Education for Women,*** New Delhi: Discovery Publishing House. ISBN 81-7141-873-2.

Bhaskara Rao, Digumarti, Digumarti Pushpa Latha and Digumarthi Harshitha, Editors (2001), ***Biological Warfare,*** New Delhi: Discovery Publishing House. ISBN 81-7141-597-0.

Bhaskara Rao, Digumarti, Digumarti Pushpa Latha and Digumarthi Harshitha, Editors (2001), ***Women as Educators,*** New Delhi: Discovery Publishing House. ISBN 81-7141-602-0.

Bhaskara Rao, Digumarti and Digumarthi Harshitha (2004), ***Adjustment of Adolescents,*** New Delhi: APH Publishing House. ISBN 81-7648-836-8.

Bhaskara Rao, Digumarti and Digumarthi Harshitha, Editors (2001), ***Education in India,*** New Delhi: APH Publishing House. ISBN 81-7648-207-2.

Bhaskara Rao, Digumarti and Digumarti Pushpa Latha, Editors (1998), ***International Encyclopaedia of Women,*** 5 Volumes, New Delhi: Discovery Publishing House. ISBN 81-7141-410-9 (set).

Vol. 1 ***Status of World's Women,*** ISBN 81-7141- 494-X.

Vol. 2 ***Women, Education and Empowerment,*** ISBN 81-7141-498-1.

Vol. 3 ***Women Challenges and Advancement,*** ISBN 81-7141-497-4.

Vol. 4 ***Women and Family Health,*** ISBN 81-7141- 497-4.

Vol. 5 ***Women and International Action,*** ISBN 81-7141-498-2.

Bhaskara Rao, Digumarti, Digumarti Pushpa Latha and Digumarthi Harshitha, Editors (2001), ***Assessing Learning Achievement,*** New Delhi: Discovery Publishing House. ISBN 81-7141-601-2.

Bhaskara Rao, Digumarti, Digumarti Pushpa Latha and Digumarthi Harshitha, Editors (2001), ***Energy Security.*** New Delhi: Discovery Publishing House. ISBN 81-7141-598-9.

Bhaskara Rao, Digumarti, Digumarthi Harshitha and K.R.S. Sambasiva Rao, Editors (1999), ***Advanced Biotechnology.*** New Delhi: Discovery Publishing House. ISBN 81-7141-516-4.

Bhaskara Rao, Digumarti and K.R.S. Sambasiva Rao, Editors (1996), ***Current Trends in Indian Education.*** New Delhi: Discovery Publishing House. ISBN 81-7141-311-0.

Bhaskara Rao, Digumarti and D. Naresh Kumar (2004), ***School Teacher Effectiveness,*** New Delhi: Discovery Publishing House. ISBN 81-7141-782-5.

Bhaskara Rao, Digumarti and E. Sreekanth Babu (2004), ***Educational Interests of School Students,*** New Delhi: Discovery Publishing House. ISBN 81-7141-837-6.

Bhaskara Rao, Digumarti and K. Vijaya (1995). ***A Text Book Evaluation,*** Ambala Cantt: The Associated Publishers.

Bhaskara Rao, Digumarti and M.A. Fayaz (2004), ***Problems of Primary School Drop-outs.*** New Delhi: Discovery Publishing House. ISBN 81-7141- 834-1.

Bhaskara Rao, Digumarti and N.V.M. Mohana Rao (2002), ***Problems of Mentally Handicapped Children,*** New Delhi: Discovery Publishing House. ISBN 81-7141- 645-4.

Bhaskara Rao, Digumarti and S. Chandra Mohan (2002), ***Sports Management,*** New Delhi: APH Publishing House. ISBN 81-7648-467-9.

Bhaskara Rao, Digumarti and S.A. Khader (2004), ***Problems of Private School Teachers,*** New Delhi: Discovery Publishing House. ISBN 81-7141-838-4.

Bhaskara Rao, Digumarti and S.A. Khader (2004), ***School Education in India,*** New Delhi: Discovery Publishing House. ISBN 81-7141-849-X.

Bhaskara Rao, Digumarti and Sk. Johni Basha (2004), ***Teachers' Population Education Awareness,*** New Delhi: Discovery Publishing House. ISBN 81-7141-832-5.

Bhaskara Rao, Digumarti, V.V. Rao, V.V. Lakshmi and V.V. Krishna, Editors (1999), ***Status and Advancement of Women,*** New Delhi: APH Publishing Corporation. ISBN 81-7648-169-6.

Appala Naidu, P.Ch., Author and Digumarti Bhaskara Rao, Editor (2007), ***Feedback Methods and Student Performance,*** New Delhi: Discovery Publishing House.

Babu, P.C., Author and Digumarti Bhaskara Rao, Editor (2004), ***Flowers of Wisdom,*** New Delhi: Discovery Publishing House. ISBN 81-7141-695-0.

Babu, Author and Digumarti Bhaskara Rao, Editor (2007), ***Teaching Aptitude of Primary School Teachers,*** New Delhi: Discovery Publishing House.

Amala, P. A. and Anupama, P., Authors and Digumarti Bhaskara Rao, Editor (2004), ***History of Education,*** New Delhi: Discovery Publishing House. ISBN 81-7141-860-0.

Bhagya Lakshmi, L., Author and Digumarti Bhaskara Rao, Editor (2000), ***Reading and Comprehension,*** New Delhi: Discovery Publishing House. ISBN 81-7141-543-1.

Bhasha, S.A., Author and Digumarti Bhaskara Rao, Editor (2004), ***Methods of Teaching Geography,*** New Delhi: Discovery Publishing House. ISBN 81-7141-807-4.

Bhuvaneswara Lakshmi, G., Author and Digumarti Bhaskara Rao, Editor (2000), ***Attitude Towards Science,*** New Delhi: Discovery Publishing House. ISBN 81-7141-541-6.

Bhuvaneswara Lakshmi, G., Author and Digumarti Bhaskara Rao, Editor (2004), ***Methods of Teaching Life Science,*** New Delhi: Discovery Publishing House. ISBN 81-7141-804-X.

Bhuvaneswara Lakshmi, G. and K. Subba Rao, Authors and Digumarti Bhaskara Rao, Editor (2004), ***Methods of Teaching Biology,*** New Delhi: Discovery Publishing House. ISBN 81-7141-914-3.

Chary, K.V.N.B., Author and Digumarti Bhaskara Rao, Editor (2006), ***Techniques of Teaching Physics,*** New Delhi: Sonali Publications. ISBN 81-8411-046-4.

Chowdary, S.B.J.R. and Naga Raju, Authors and Digumarti Bhaskara Rao, Editor (2004), ***Mastery of Teaching Skills,*** New Delhi: Discovery Publishing House.

Dayakara Reddy, V. and Digumarti Bhaskara Rao, Editors (2006), ***Value-Oriented Education,*** New Delhi: Discovery Publishing House.

Devraj, T.A.S., Author and Digumarti Bhaskara Rao, Editor (1997), ***Trace Analysis of Uranium and Thorium,*** New Delhi: Discovery Publishing House. ISBN 81-7141-375-7.

Durga Rani, K., Author and Digumarti Bhaskara Rao, Editor (2000), ***Educational Aspirations and Scientific Attitudes,*** New Delhi: Discovery Publishing House. ISBN 81-7141-555-5.

Dutt, B.S.V. and Digumarti Bhaskara Rao (2001), ***Empowering Primary Teachers,*** New Delhi: Discovery Publishing House. ISBN 81-7141-615-2.

Dutt, B.S.V., Author and Digumarti Bhaskara Rao, Editor (2004), ***Comparative Education,*** New Delhi: Discovery Publishing House. ISBN 81-7141-912-7.

Ediger, Marlow and Digumarti Bhaskara Rao (1996), ***Science Curriculum,*** New Delhi: Discovery Publishing House. ISBN 81-7141-321-8.

Ediger, Marlow and Digumarti Bhaskara Rao (2000), ***Teaching Mathematics Successfully,*** New Delhi: Discovery Publishing House. ISBN 81-7141-552-0.

Ediger, Marlow and Digumarti Bhaskara Rao (2001), ***Teaching Science Successfully,*** New Delhi: Discovery Publishing House. ISBN 81-7141-600-4.

Ediger, Marlow and Digumarti Bhaskara Rao (2001), ***Teaching Social Studies Successfully,*** New Delhi: Discovery Publishing House. ISBN 81-7141-596-2.

Ediger, Marlow and Digumarti Bhaskara Rao (2002), ***Philosophy and Curriculum,*** New Delhi: Discovery Publishing House. ISBN 81-7141-631-4.

Ediger, Marlow and Digumarti Bhaskara Rao (2002), ***Improving School Administration,*** New Delhi: Discovery Publishing House. ISBN 81-7141-633-0.

Ediger, Marlow and Digumarti Bhaskara Rao (2002), ***Elementary Curriculum,*** New Delhi: Discovery Publishing House. ISBN 81-7141-658-6.

Ediger, Marlow and Digumarti Bhaskara Rao (2003), ***Language Arts Curriculum,*** New Delhi: Discovery Publishing House. ISBN 81-7141-657-8.

Ediger, Marlow and Digumarti Bhaskara Rao (2003), ***Psychology and Curriculum,*** New Delhi: Discovery Publishing House. ISBN 81-7141-691-8.

Ediger, Marlow and Digumarti Bhaskara Rao (2003), ***Teaching Language Arts Successfully,*** New Delhi: Discovery Publishing House. ISBN 81-7141-678-0.

Ediger, Marlow and Digumarti Bhaskara Rao (2003), ***School Curriculum and Administration,*** New Delhi: Discovery Publishing House. ISBN 81-7141-709-4.

Ediger, Marlow and Digumarti Bhaskara Rao (2003), ***Teaching Mathematics in Elementary Schools,*** New Delhi: Discovery Publishing House. ISBN 81-7141-687-X.

Ediger, Marlow and Digumarti Bhaskara Rao (2003), ***Teaching Science in Elementary Schools,*** New Delhi: Discovery Publishing House. ISBN 81-7141-698-5.

Ediger, Marlow and Digumarti Bhaskara Rao (2003), ***School Curriculum and Administration,*** New Delhi: Discovery Publishing House. ISBN 81-7141-709-4.

Ediger, Marlow and Digumarti Bhaskara Rao (2003), ***Elementary Curriculum Improvement,*** New Delhi: Discovery Publishing House. ISBN 81-7141-740-X.

Ediger, Marlow and Digumarti Bhaskara Rao (2004), ***Modern Elementary School,*** New Delhi: Discovery Publishing House.

Ediger, Marlow and Digumarti Bhaskara Rao (2004), ***School Organisation,*** New Delhi: Discovery Publishing House. ISBN 81-7141-843-0.

Ediger, Marlow and Digumarti Bhaskara Rao (2004), ***Relevancy in Elementary Curriculum,*** New Delhi: Discovery Publishing House. ISBN 81-7141-845-9.

Ediger, Marlow and Digumarti Bhaskara Rao (2005), ***Quality School Education,*** New Delhi: Discovery Publishing House. ISBN 81-8356-022-9.

Ediger, Marlow and Digumarti Bhaskara Rao (2006), ***Successful School Education,*** New Delhi: Discovery Publishing House. ISBN 81-8356-054-7.

Ediger, Marlow and Digumarti Bhaskara Rao (2006), ***Successful School Administration,*** New Delhi: Discovery Publishing House. ISBN 81-8356-046-6.

Ediger, Marlow and Digumarti Bhaskara Rao (2006), ***Issues in School Curriculum,*** New Delhi: Discovery Publishing House. ISBN 81-8356-052-0.

Ediger, Marlow and Digumarti Bhaskara Rao (2006), ***Community College – Curriculum and Teaching,*** New Delhi: Discovery Publishing House. ISBN 81-8356-053-9.

Ediger, Marlow and Digumarti Bhaskara Rao (2006), ***Administration of Schools,*** New Delhi: Discovery Publishing House.

Ediger, Marlow and Digumarti Bhaskara Rao (2006), ***Reading Curriculum and Instruction,*** New Delhi: Discovery Publishing House.

Ediger, Marlow and Digumarti Bhaskara Rao (2006), ***Curriculum Organisation,*** New Delhi: Discovery Publishing House.

Ediger, Marlow and Digumarti Bhaskara Rao (2006), ***Curriculum of School Subjects,*** New Delhi: Discovery Publishing House.

Ediger, Marlow, B.S.V. Dutt and Digumarti Bhaskara Rao (2003), ***Teaching English Successfully,*** New Delhi: Discovery Publishing House. ISBN 81-7141-707-8.

Elizabeth, M.E.S., Author and Digumarti Bhaskara Rao, Editor (2004), ***Methods of Teaching English,*** New Delhi: Discovery Publishing House. ISBN 81-7141-809-0.

Elizabeth, M.E.S., author and Digumarti Bhaskara Rao, Editor (2004), ***Acquisition of English Vocabulary,*** New Delhi: Discovery Publishing House. ISBN 81-8356-075-X.

Fatima, Sk. Author and Digumarti Bhaskara Rao, Editor (2007), ***Reasoning Ability of School Students,*** New Delhi: Discovery Publishing House.

Harshitha, Digumarthi, Author and Digumarti Bhaskara Rao, Editor (2004), ***Methods of Teaching Information Technology,*** New Delhi: Discovery Publishing House. ISBN 81-7141-805-8.

Indira Devi, author and J. Prasanth Kumar and Digumarti Bhaskara Rao, Editors (2004), ***Values in Language Text Books,*** New Delhi: Discovery Publishing House.

Jalaja Kumari, C., Author and Digumarti Bhaskara Rao, Editor (2004), ***Methods of Teaching Educational Technology,*** New Delhi: Discovery Publishing House. ISBN 81-7141-810-4.

Jalaja Kumari, C., Author and Digumarti Bhaskara Rao, Editor (2007), ***Job Satisfaction of Teachers,*** New Delhi: Discovery Publishing House.

Janardhan Reddy, B., Author and Digumarti Bhaskara Rao, Editor (2006), ***Techniques of Teaching Sociology,*** New Delhi: Sonali Publications. ISBN 81-8411-042-1.

Jayasree, K., Author and Digumarti Bhaskara Rao, Editor (1999), ***Correlates of Socialisation,*** New Delhi: Discovery Publishing House. ISBN 81-7141-517-2.

Jayasree, K., Author and Digumarti Bhaskara Rao, Editor (2004). ***Methods of Teaching Science,*** New Delhi: Discovery Publishing House. ISBN 81-7141-801-5.

John Babu, C., Author and T.J.R. Prasad, G.M. Madhukar and Digumarti Bhaskara Rao, Editors (1996), **Problem Solving in Mathematics,** New Delhi: APH Publishing Corporation. ISBN 81-7648-273-0.

Joseph Raju, B and G.A. Anitha, Authors and Digumarti Bhaskara Rao, Editor (2004), ***Population Education,*** New Delhi: Sonali Publications. ISBN 81-88836-31-3.

Lalitha, T., Author and K.S. Prabhakaram, D.S.N. Sastry and Digumarti Bhaskara Rao, Editors (2004), ***Educational Philosophic Beliefs,*** New Delhi: Discovery Publishing House. ISBN 81-7141-765-5.

Krishna, G., Author and Digumarti Bhaskara Rao, editor (2006), ***Techniques of Teaching Physical Education,*** New Delhi: Sonali Publications. ISBN 81-8411-044-8.

Lakshmi Kumari, V., Author and Digumarti Bhaskara Rao, Editor (2006), ***Techniques of Teaching Home Science,*** New Delhi: Sonali Publications. ISBN 81-8411-048-0.

Madhu Bala, Jampala, Author and Digumarti Bhaskara Rao, Editor (2004), ***Adjustment Problems of Hearing Impaired,*** New Delhi: Discovery Publishing House. ISBN 81-7141-831-7.

Madhu Bala, Jampala, Author and Digumarti Bhaskara Rao, Editor (2004), ***Methods of Teaching Exceptional Children,*** New Delhi: Discovery Publishing House. ISBN 81-7141-802-3.

Madhu Bala, Jampala, Author and Digumarti Bhaskara Rao, Editor (2007), ***Adjustment, Problems of Hearing Impaired,*** New Delhi: Discovery Publishing House

Marja, Talvi and Digumarti Bhaskara Rao, Editors (1996), ***Educational Leadership and Social Changes,*** New Delhi: Discovery Publishing House. ISBN 81-7141-320-X.

Nageswara Rao, S. and M. Srihari, Authors and Digumarti Bhaskara Rao, Editor (2004), ***Guidance and Counselling,*** New Delhi: Discovery Publishing House. ISBN 81-7141-840-6

Nageswara Rao, S., Author and Digumarti Bhaskara Rao, Editor (2006), ***Techniques of Teaching Psychology,*** New Delhi: Sonali Publications. ISBN 81-8411-040-5.

Nageswara Rao, S. and P. Sridhar, Authors and Digumarti Bhaskara Rao, Editor (2004), ***Methods and Techniques of Teaching,*** New Delhi: Sonali Publications.ISBN 81-88836-33-8.

Nirmala Jyothi, M., Author and Digumarti Bhaskara Rao, Editor (2003), ***Non-detention System in School Education,*** New Delhi: Discovery Publishing House. ISBN 81-7141-654-3.

Padma Tulasi, G., Author and Digumarti Bhaskara Rao, Editor (2004), ***Methods of Teaching Elementary Science,*** New Delhi: Discovery Publishing House. ISBN 81-7141-871-6.

Prasad Babu, B., Author and P. Madhu and Digumarti Bhaskara Rao, Editors (2006), **Psychological Adjustment and Well-being,** New Delhi: Discovery Publishing House.

Prasad Babu, B., Author and M.V.R. Raju and Digumarti Bhaskara Rao, Editors (2006), ***Behavioural Problems of School Children,*** New Delhi: Discovery Publishing House.

Prasada Rao, V.P., Author and K. N. Rani and D. Bhaskara Rao, Editors (2004), ***India Pakistan: Partition Perspectives in Indo English Novels,*** New Delhi: Discovery Publishing House. ISBN 81-7141-871-6.

Prasada Rao, V.P. and D. Bhaskara Rao, Editors (2008). ***Functioning of Autonomous Colleges,*** New Delhi: Discovery Publishing House.

Prabhakaram, K.S., Author and Digumarti Bhaskara Rao, Editor (1998), ***Concept Attainment Model in Mathematics Teaching,*** New Delhi: Discovery Publishing House. ISBN 81-7141-424-9.

Prasanth Kumar, J., Author and Digumarti Bhaskara Rao, Editor (1998), ***Effectiveness of Distance Education System,*** New Delhi: Discovery Publishing House. ISBN 81-7141-437-0.

Prasanth Kumar, J., Author and Digumarti Bhaskara Rao, Editor (2004), ***Methods of Teaching Civics,*** New Delhi: Discovery Publishing House. ISBN 81-7141-806-6.

Prasanth Kumar, J., Author and G. Sundara Rao and Digumarti Bhaskara Rao, Editors (2000), ***Open University Student Support Services,*** New Delhi: Discovery Publishing House. ISBN 81-7141-550-4.

Raja Kumari, M.A. and D.R.S. Sundari, Authors and Digumarti Bhaskara Rao, Editor (2004), ***Special Education,*** New Delhi: Discovery Publishing House. ISBN 81-7141-846-5.

Raja Kumari, M.A. and D.R.S. Sundari, Authors and Digumarti Bhaskara Rao, Editor (2004), ***Methods of Teaching Educational Psychology,*** New Delhi: Discovery Publishing House. ISBN 81-7141-820-1.

Ramatulasamma, K., Author and Digumarti Bhaskara Rao, Editor (2002), ***Job Satisfaction of Teacher Educators,*** New Delhi: Discovery Publishing House. ISBN 81-7141-655-1.

Rama Krishnaiah, D., Author and Digumarti Bhaskara Rao, Editor (1998), ***Job Satisfaction of College Teachers,*** New Delhi: Discovery Publishing House. ISBN 81-7141-438-9.

Rama Kumar Ratnam, M.V., Author and Digumarti Bhaskara Rao, Editor (1998), ***Dukkha: Suffering in Early Buddhism.*** New Delhi: Discovery Publishing House. ISBN 81-7141-653-5.

Rama Krishna Prasad and P. Vidya Sagar, Authors and Digumarti Bhaskara Rao, Editor (2004), ***Methods of Teaching Physical Education,*** New Delhi: Discovery Publishing House.

Rama Seshaiah, P., Author and Digumarti Bhaskara Rao, Editor (2004). ***Methods of Teaching Home Science,*** New Delhi: Discovery Publishing House. ISBN 81-7141-916-X.

Ramesh, A.R., Author and Digumarti Bhaskara Rao, Editor (2006). ***Techniques of Teaching Commerce,*** New Delhi: Sonali Publications. ISBN 81-8411-036-7.

Ramesh, Ghanta and Digumarti Bhaskara Rao, Editors (1998), ***Environmental Education: Problems and Prospects,*** New Delhi: Discovery Publishing House. ISBN 81-7141-423-0.

Ranga Rao, R., Author and Digumarti Bhaskara Rao, Editor (2004), ***Methods of Teacher Teaching,*** New Delhi: Discovery Publishing House. ISBN 81-7141-812-0.

Rani, S.S., Author and Digumarti Bhaskara Rao, Editor (2006), ***Techniques of Teaching Botany,*** New Delhi: Sonali Publications. ISBN 81-8411-037-5.

Rathaiah, Lavu and Digumarti Bhaskara Rao, Editors (1996), ***International Innovations in Education,*** New Delhi: Discovery Publishing House. ISBN 81-7141-359-5.

Rathaiah, Lavu and Digumarti Bhaskara Rao (1997), ***Achievement Correlates,*** New Delhi: Discovery Publishing House. ISBN 81-7141- 385-4.

Ravi Krishna, M., Author and Digumarti Bhaskara Rao, Editor (2004), ***Examination System,*** New Delhi: Discovery Publishing House. ISBN 81-7141-824-4.

Ravi Kumar, M., Author and Digumarti Bhaskara Rao, Editor (2004), ***Methods of Teaching Computer Science,*** New Delhi: Discovery Publishing House. ISBN 81-7141-823-6.

Rudramamba, B., Author and Digumarti Bhaskara Rao, Editor (2003), ***Problems of Teaching,*** New Delhi: APH Publishing Corporation. ISBN 81-7648-462-8.

Rudramamba, B. and V. Lakshmi Kumari, Authors and Digumarti Bhaskara Rao, Editor (2004), ***Methods of Teaching Economics***, New Delhi: Discovery Publishing House. ISBN 81-7141-900-3.

Sanjeeva Rao, P.C., Author and Digumarti Bhaskara Rao, Editor (1996), ***A Text Book of Geology***, New Delhi: Discovery Publishing House. ISBN 81-7141-313-7.

Sarala, M.M.O., Author and Digumarti Bhaskara Rao, Editor (2006), ***Techniques of Teaching English***, New Delhi: Sonali Publications. ISBN 81-8411-047-2.

Satya Narayana, V., Author and Digumarti Bhaskara Rao, Editor (2001), ***Physical Education, Social Attitudes and Leadership Qualities***, New Delhi: Discovery Publishing House. ISBN 81-7141-593-8.

Satya Narayana, P.V.V. and G. Krishna, Authors and Digumarti Bhaskara Rao, Editor (2004), ***Curriculum Development and Management***, New Delhi: Discovery Publishing House. ISBN 81-7141-813-9.

Shamsuddin, Sk. and V. Dayakara Reddy, Authors and Digumarti Bhaskara Rao, Editor (2007), ***Academic Achievement and Values***, New Delhi: Discovery Publishing House.

Singh, Y.C., Author and Digumarti Bhaskara Rao, Editor (2006), **Techniques of Teaching Science**, New Delhi: Sonali Publications. ISBN 81-8411-042-3.

Sivaratnam Reddy, M., Author and Digumarti Bhaskara Rao, Editor (2004), ***Creativity in College Students***, New Delhi: Discovery Publishing House. ISBN 81-7141-697-7.

Siva Lakshmi, G.V. and G.L. Subbaiah, Authors and Digumarti Bhaskara Rao, Editor (2004), ***Methods of Teaching Environmental Science***, New Delhi: Discovery Publishing House. ISBN 81-7141-839-2.

Srinivas, M. and I. Prasada Rao, Authors and Digumarti Bhaskara Rao, Editor (2004), ***Methods of Teaching History***, New Delhi: Discovery Publishing House. ISBN 81-7141-803-1.

Srinivasulu Reddy, M. and K.R.S. Sambasiva Rao, Authors and Digumarti Bhaskara Rao, Editor (1999), ***A Text Book of Aquaculture,*** New Delhi: Discovery Publishing House. ISBN 81-7141-482-6.

Srinivasa Rao, Mandalapu, Author and Digumarti Bhaskara Rao, Editor (2003), ***Achievement Motivation and Achievement in Mathematics,*** New Delhi: Discovery Publishing House. ISBN 81-7141-674-8.

Srihari, M., Author and Digumarti Bhaskara Rao, Editor (2003), ***Values of Prospective Teachers,*** New Delhi: Discovery Publishing House.

Subba Rao, K., Author and Digumarti Bhaskara Rao, Editor (2007), ***School Education Policy,*** New Delhi: Discovery Publishing House.

Sudhakar Reddy, Y., Author and Digumarti Bhaskara Rao, Editor (2003), ***Creativity in Adolescents,*** New Delhi: Discovery Publishing House. ISBN 81-7141-659-4.

Sunil Kumar, K. and K. Rama Krishana, Authors and Digumarti Bhaskara Rao, Editor (2004), ***Methods of Teaching Chemistry.*** New Delhi: Discovery Publishing House. ISBN 81-7141-913-5.

Sunita, E. and R. Sambasiva Rao, Authors and Digumarti Bhaskara Rao, Editor (2004), ***Methods of Teaching Mathematics,*** New Delhi: Discovery Publishing House. ISBN 81-7141-915-1.

Surya Madhava, I., Author and Digumarti Bhaskara Rao, Editor (2006), ***Techniques of Teaching Geography,*** New Delhi: Sonali Publications. ISBN 81-8411-034-0.

Swamy, K.R., Author and Digumarti Bhaskara Rao, Editor (2006), ***Techniques of Teaching Environmental Science,*** New Delhi: Sonali Publications. ISBN 81-8411-035-9.

Swarna Latha, C.D., and Digumarti Bhaskara Rao, Editors (2006), ***Encyclopaedia of Biotechnology,*** 5 Volumes, New Delhi: Discovery Publishing House. ISBN 81-8356-168-3. (set).

Swarupa Rani, T. and J.R. Priyadarshini, Authors and Digumarti Bhaskara Rao, Editor (2004), ***Educational Measurement and Evaluation,*** New Delhi: Discovery Publishing House. ISBN 81-7141-859-7.

Vanaja, M., Author and Digumarti Bhaskara Rao, Editor (1999), ***Inquiry Training Model,*** New Delhi: Discovery Publishing House. ISBN 81-7141-515-6.

Vanaja, M., Author and Digumarti Bhaskara Rao, Editor (2004), ***Methods of Teaching Physics,*** New Delhi: Discovery Publishing House. ISBN 81-7141-867-8.

Valeri V. Koustiouk, Author and Digumarti Bhaskara Rao, Editor (2002), ***A Text Book of Cryogenics,*** New Delhi: Discovery Publishing House. ISBN 81-7141-642-X.

Vamsi Krishna, V., Author and Digumarti Bhaskara Rao, Editor (2004), ***School Psychology.*** New Delhi: Discovery Publishing House. ISBN 81-7141-880-5.

Veena Kumari, Balusu and Digumarti Bhaskara Rao (1996), ***Operation Black Board,*** New Delhi: APH Publishing Corporation. ISBN 81-7024-711-X.

Veena Kumari, Balusu, Author and Digumarti Bhaskara Rao, Editor (2004), ***Methods of Teaching Social Studies.*** New Delhi: Discovery Publishing House. ISBN 81-7141-899-6.

Veena Kumari, Balusu, Author and Digumarti Bhaskara Rao, Editor (2000), ***Psycho-Social Correlates of Achievement.*** New Delhi: Discovery Publishing House. ISBN 81-7141-547-4.

Venkata Rao, P. and Digumarti Bhaskara Rao (1989), ***A Text Book of Zoology–Junior Intermediate,*** Guntur: Vignan Publishers.

Venkata Rao, P. and Digumarti Bhaskara Rao (1989), ***A Text Book of Zoology–Senior Intermediate,*** Guntur: Vignan Publishers.

Venkateswara Rao, V., Author and Digumarti Bhaskara Rao, Editor (2004), ***Problems of Education,*** New Delhi: Discovery Publishing House. ISBN 81-7141-841-4.

Venkateswara Rao, V., V. Vijaya Lakshmi and V. Vamsi Krishna, Authors and Digumarti Bhaskara Rao, Editor (2004), ***Education For All,*** New Delhi: Sonali Publications. ISBN 81-88836-30-3.

Venkateswara Rao, V., V. Vijaya Lakshmi and V. Vamsi Krishna, Authors and Digumarti Bhaskara Rao, Editor (2004), ***Education in India,*** New Delhi: Sonali Publications. ISBN 81-88836-858-9.

Venkateswara Reddy, L. and Narayana, M. L., Authors and Digumarti Bhaskara Rao, Editor (2004), ***Education for Dalits,*** New Delhi: Discovery Publishing House. ISBN 81-7141-872-4.

Venkateswara Reddy, L. and Narayana, M.L, Authors and Digumarti Bhaskara Rao, Editor (2004), ***Methods of Teaching Rural Sociology,*** New Delhi: Discovery Publishing House. ISBN 81-7141-811-2.

Venkateswarlu, K. and S.J. Basha, Authors and Digumarti Bhaskara Rao, Editor (2004), ***Methods of Teaching Commerce,*** New Delhi: Discovery Publishing House. ISBN 81-7141-808-2.

Venugopala Rao, K., Author and Digumarti Bhaskara Rao, Editor (2000), ***Teacher Morale in Secondary Schools,*** New Delhi: Discovery Publishing House. ISBN 81-7141-551-2.

Vimala, T.D., B. Prasada Babu and Digumarti Bhaskara Rao, Editors (2007), ***Stress, Coping and Management,*** New Delhi: Sonali Publications. ISBN 81-8411-086-3.

Vidya, C., Author and Digumarti Bhaskara Rao, Editor (1996), ***A Text Book of Nutrition,*** New Delhi: Discovery Publishing House. ISBN 81-7141-309-9.

Vijaya Bharathi, D., Author and Digumarti Bhaskara Rao, Editor (2000), ***Educational Philosophies of Swami Vivekananda and John Dewey,*** New Delhi: APH Publishing House. ISBN 81-7648-309-9.

Vijaya Bharathi, D., Author and Digumarti Bhaskara Rao, Editor (2005), ***Educational Philosophy of John Dewey.*** New Delhi: Discovery Publishing House. ISBN 81-8356-024-5.

Vijaya Bharathi, D., Author and Digumarti Bhaskara Rao, Editor (2005), ***Educational Philosophy of Swami Vivekananda,*** New Delhi: Discovery Publishing House. ISBN 81-8356-023-7.

Vijaya Lakshmi, D., Author and Digumarti Bhaskara Rao, Editor (2004), ***Basic Education.*** New Delhi: Discovery Publishing House. ISBN 81-7141-881-3.

Vijaya Lakshmi, V., Author and Digumarti Bhaskara Rao, Editor (2006), ***Techniques of Teaching Music,*** New Delhi: Sonali Publications. ISBN 81-8411-038-3.

Vijaya Kumar, S.J., Author and Digumarti Bhaskara Rao, Editor (2006), ***Techniques of Teaching Mathematics,*** New Delhi: Discovery Publishing House. ISBN 81-8411-039-1.

Visalakshi, V., Author and Digumarti Bhaskara Rao, Editor (2006), ***Techniques of Teaching Biology,*** New Delhi: Sonali Publications. ISBN 81-8411-045-6.

INDEX

R

S

T